Praise for (

"Binge eating disorder is the most [...] stood of all eating disorders, but *Crave* unlocks the mystery of this debilitating condition and offers essential, clinically proven strategies for recovery. Chock-full of up-to-the-minute science, supportive encouragement, and true life stories, this book is a must-read if you've ever struggled with out-of-control eating or the weight gain so often associated with binge eating disorder."

—Aimee Liu, author of *Gaining: The Truth About Life After Eating Disorders*

"As both former secretary of Health and Human Services and someone with a close connection to this subject, I am professionally and personally aware of the importance of providing education about eating difficulties that can have an enormous and widespread impact on individuals and their loved ones. I applaud Dr. Bulik for tackling this complex subject in a practical, sensitive, and supportive way."

—Tommy G. Thompson

"Dr. Bulik's no-nonsense, easy-to-read, respectful, and clear approach is refreshing. *Crave* helps us all to better understand the illness while providing concrete tools and hope for a successful recovery."

—Lynn S. Grefe, chief executive officer of the National Eating Disorders Association

"It's about time that we get the devastating problem of binge eating disorder out of the closet. In *Crave*, Dr. Bulik has done just that. A prolific researcher and dedicated clinician with decades of experience, she translates sophisticated scientific and clinical information into plain and easily understood language. The result is a practical guide to identifying binge eating, understanding its multiple biological, environmental, and psychological roots, and developing individualized strategies to change these behaviors and restore a sense of well-being and personal empowerment. *Crave* will not only help the millions of Americans struggling with binge eating, but it can also equip both their loved ones and health care professionals with the most current information and innovative solutions. Bulik's straight talk, engaging examples, and compassionate approach may break the pattern of isolation, hopelessness, and deep shame that keeps so many imprisoned in the binge eating cycle."

—Margo Maine, Ph.D., fellow of the Academy of Eating Disorders, coauthor of *The Body Myth,* and author of *Father Hunger* and *Body Wars*

"*Crave* offers access to extraordinary clinical wisdom without the clinical distance. With lively language and a gift for relevant metaphor, Dr. Bulik draws together the science and practice of eating disorder treatment for binge eating—an important and underserved issue."

—Laura Collins, director of Families Empowered and Supporting Treatment of Eating Disorders

"In *Crave*, Dr. Bulik empowers people who struggle with binge eating disorder to take action. She uses her knowledge, experience, and wisdom to help us understand binge eating disorder and what can be done about it. Dr. Bulik offers much needed hope to the millions of people who struggle with binge eating disorder by giving very practical and time-tested strategies while dispelling the myths and misconceptions surrounding all eating disorders. She offers her incredible insight and knowledge of eating disorders with compassion and understanding in order to help people reach the ultimate goal: Success. Thank you, Dr. Bulik, for this amazing book."

—Kitty Westin, president of the Eating Disorders Coalition for Research, Policy and Action

crave

By the same author

Runaway Eating: The 8-Point Plan to Conquer Adult Food and Weight Obsessions with Nadine Taylor, M.S., R.D.

Eating Disorders: Detection and Treatment

crave

WHY YOU BINGE EAT
AND HOW TO STOP

Cynthia M. Bulik, Ph.D.

WALKER & COMPANY
NEW YORK

Published by Walker Publishing Company, Inc., New York

All papers used by Walker & Company are natural, recyclable products
made from wood grown in well-managed forests. The manufacturing pro-
cesses conform to the environmental regulations of the country of origin.

Excerpt from *Feed Me!: Writers Dish About Food, Eating, Weight,
and Body Image* reprinted with permission.

LIBRARY OF CONGRESS CATALOGING-IN-PUBLICATION DATA
Bulik, Cynthia M.
Crave: why you binge eat and how to stop/Cynthia M. Bulik.—1st U.S. ed.
p. cm.
ISBN-13: 978-0-8027-1710-8
ISBN-10: 0-8027-1710-1
1. Compulsive eating—Popular works. I. Title.

RC552.C65B847 2009
616.85'26—dc22
2008032192

Visit Walker & Company's Web site at www.walkerbooks.com

First U.S. edition 2009

3 5 7 9 10 8 6 4 2

Designed by Rachel Reiss

Typeset by Westchester Book Group
Printed in the United States of America by Quebecor World Fairfield

This book is dedicated to my family, who understands and supports my passion and my science, and to the countless advocates who are fighting on many fronts to destigmatize eating disorders so that they can have the recognition, funding, and insurance coverage they deserve.

Contents

Satisfying Your Craving for Relief

Binge eating tops the list of eating disorders affecting Americans, with the first-ever national survey on eating disorders finding it much more prevalent than either anorexia or bulimia.

—HEALTHDAY NEWS

It's a common scenario played out in millions of households around the country every single day: A woman eats her favorite ice cream straight from the carton until she reaches the bottom, or a man goes to his favorite sports bar and practically inhales twenty buffalo wings. Each is simply trying to satisfy intense, at times overwhelming, cravings. Some crave sweets, others pasta; whatever the target, it finds its way from hand to mouth.

Every binge is different, just as every craving is different and every binge eater is different, but the scenario is most often the same: Binge eaters like to be alone with their behavior, often turning to late-night, early-morning, or even what I call "backseat" binges to ensure that no one sees their so-called shameful activities, those times when the kids are asleep, the parents are out of town, the spouse is still at work, or the roommate has just left for that big business trip or is still taking her final exams.

My patients have told me countless horror stories of how far they went to conceal a binge: driving across city, county, or even state lines so no one they know will witness them going from fast-food restaurant to convenience store, or from drive-through to drive-through in record time. Some have even hidden in a closet with a grocery bag full of clandestine food.

Those willing to look a little beyond the carefully constructed façade might notice some telltale signs of a classic binge eater: snack-cake wrappers wedged between sofa cushions, caches of food hidden throughout the house, fast-food receipts stacked like Monopoly money in car glove compartments, and greasy wrappers littering the floorboards. But not everyone leaves a trail; some binge eaters spend as much time covering their tracks as they do shopping for the binge itself.

Regardless, the cravings can seem insatiable. Day or night, alone or with someone just in the next room, the binge eater can hardly refuse the cravings that cause him or her to ingest five hundred, a thousand, or even sometimes as many as five thousand or more calories in a single sitting.

The urges to eat are often as intense as they are spontaneous; later in this book we will talk about what triggers a mere craving or a full-fledged binge episode, but patients have told me that when it happens, for whatever reason, they feel powerless to resist the urge and often "zone out" while eating. So while the initial craving may be for food from a certain food group, restaurant, snack bar, or doughnut shop, what happens during the binge itself has very little to do with taste.

Recently a colleague of mine confessed to me that she was concerned that her husband might be a closet binge eater. When I asked her why she thought that, she admitted that she had caught him feasting on saltine crackers and mayonnaise in the middle of the night!

Clearly, binge eating is not merely the occasional craving of someone who's hungry, who may consume a handful of chips or a single doughnut. Binge eating involves the supersizing of cravings to the point of an uncontrollable urge that snowballs until the binge eater literally feels helpless to resist the urge to binge.

Binge eaters don't just consume a handful of potato chips; they'll down a whole bag in a sitting—and that may be just a teaser for the grand finale that's to come. A bowl of ice cream may be just the appetizer for the whole pint—and then another, if it's handy or if there's a convenience store within easy driving distance. A single doughnut? Forget it; the binge eater wants six and, stomach swollen, blood sugar skyrocketing, will contemplate getting in the car and heading to the nearest drive-through to make it an even dozen.

Binge eating disorder is classified by a distinct and measurable *pattern of behavior* that has manifested itself in the individual's life, often over many months or years. Does this sound like someone you know or love?

Maybe a lot like . . . *you*?

Then we're both right where we're supposed to be. My name is Cynthia Bulik, Ph.D., and I am the director of the Eating Disorders Program at the University of North Carolina at Chapel Hill. It is my mission to inform as many people as possible about the dangers of binge eating, to help those who already feel trapped to escape, and to prevent others from falling into the dangerous cycle of binge eating. Be it prevention or treatment, success is my ultimate goal.

As so often happens in the field of medicine, my interest in binge eating came about through a combination of happenstance and career path. After receiving my bachelor's degree from the University of Notre Dame and my master's degree and doctorate from the University of California at Berkeley, I became interested in eating disorders while researching childhood depression. Mood and food are so intricately intertwined, and it seemed whenever I was doing research on depression I was reading about appetite and weight, and whenever I was working on eating disorders, I was hearing about depression and anxiety. We know these systems are linked in our psychology, but we are now discovering that they are also linked in our biology.

Why You Binge Eat—And How to Stop

If you are a binge eater you're not alone, not anymore. Thanks to decades of research in the field, hundreds of patient case studies, and reams of research conducted on this very topic, I have the resources to help you get the upper hand on your own binge eating, and together we can conquer the problem.

Binge eating disorder is a highly treatable condition. When we give patients behavioral tools to "curb the crave" at our program at UNC, most of those who use them can—and do—triumph over their binge eating. You will hear about these patients, men and women, young and old, and how they conquered their disorder using a variety of strategies in their personal arsenal; you will learn these strategies as well.

What about gaining weight? I know how closely linked concerns over weight and binge eating are, and that is why for anyone trying to get control over their binge eating losing weight and keeping it off are a critical part of both treatment and self-discovery. Once you can to identify the causes of your cravings, it becomes easier to lose weight as well as to bring your binges under control.

Across the country, many effective forms of treatment exist to help sufferers overcome their disorder, including:

- Counseling and psychotherapy
- Medication
- Self-help programs

- Nutrition counseling
- Behavioral weight-control programs

Specific treatment programs will be discussed later, but I wanted to introduce them early so you know that effective options do exist, and many may be well within your reach. Whatever form of treatment you seek for yourself—or for others—rest assured that right now, by following the guidelines in this book, you are taking the first critical step toward getting help.

I deal with people every day who are going through what you are going through. I know firsthand how much courage it takes to first of all admit there is a problem and second, address the problem with specific, safe, and effective steps toward long-term recovery.

There is nothing fancy about my approach. In fact it is down to earth, user friendly, and very practical. Strategies to "curb the crave" include surprisingly simple methods you will soon be able to implement in your daily routine:

- Eat breakfast, hungry or not
- Don't drink your meals
- Beware of stealth sugars
- Retrain your taste buds
- Computer-track your cravings
- Use instant messaging and texting for reinforcement
- Do lunch laps, mall marches, and other exercise

My research and the latest studies done by colleagues in the field reveal how our genes can put some of us at greater risk for binge eating and its almost universal by-product, obesity. However, this research has also proven one reassuring fact: No one needs to be a prisoner of his or her genes any longer; everyone can learn to make better eating decisions and control his or her diet on a lifelong basis.

But the solution has to be personalized. A generic, cookie-cutter approach won't work. You have to identify the "crave-ology" profile that gibes most with your experience and select the tools that work best for you. Some typical binge-eating pro-files include:

- the Moody Blues Binger
- the Angry Binger
- the Low Self-Esteem Binger
- the Nail-Biting Binger
- the Running-on-Empty Binger
- the Bedroom Binger
- the Midnight Binger
- the Drive-Through Binger
- the Party Hearty Binger
- the Buffet Binger

Maybe some of these will sound familiar right off the bat, while others require further explanation. You may identify your-self as one type or a combination, or you may feel like "all of the above." However you decide to classify yourself, I urge you to use this book as your toolbox; these are the tools you can use to help yourself—or help a friend, family member, or loved one—recover from binge eating disorder. A special section in chapter 9 lists resources where you can get information and referrals. They can help; I can help; most of all, you can help yourself triumph over binge eating disorder.

PART I

Curb the Crave

Whether you're a soccer mom with a bag of candy bars in the glove compartment, a soccer coach concerned about one of the players on your team, or a soccer player struggling to be stronger and leaner than anyone else on the squad, you don't have to be a slave to your cravings anymore.

CHAPTER 1

One in Thirty-five
Binge Eating Disorder Is Widespread in America

One night, after a particularly destructive binge, I became desperate. I was no longer in control of my food, it was controlling me, and I felt I could not go on living that way. I contemplated ending my life as the only way out of my entrapment by food. But I was still rational enough to reach out for help.
—JANE E. BRODY, *FEED ME!: WRITERS DISH ABOUT FOOD, EATING, BODY IMAGE, AND WEIGHT*[1]

Scientists have known about overeating and binge eating for decades, but only now are these conditions getting the attention they so rightfully merit. In 2007 a new U.S. study of eating disorders reported that binge eating disorder, not yet officially recognized as a psychiatric illness, is more common than anorexia or bulimia nervosa. This study revealed that binge eating disorder occurs in about one in thirty-five adults in this country.

This landmark study, first reported in the February 1 issue of *Biological Psychiatry*, details how researchers at Harvard University surveyed nearly 3,000 participants in a population-based study to determine a variety of relevant, pertinent, and timely facts about eating disorders.[2] In the study, which was picked up by the press worldwide, researchers discovered that 0.6 percent of their participants suffered from anorexia nervosa, 1 percent from bulimia nervosa, and *2.8 percent from binge eating disorder.* When we break that down by gender, the numbers are even more staggering: 3.5 percent of American women over the age of eighteen and 2 percent of men report suffering from binge eating disorder. Translated into real numbers, that means that approximately 5,250,000 women and 3,000,000 men in America suffer from binge eating disorder.

According to the National Institute of Mental Health (NIMH), the researchers also noted that binge eating disorder "should be considered a public health concern because symptoms of the illness appear to be more prevalent than other eating disorders, and it is strongly associated with obesity."[3]

This first large-scale study in the United States clearly demonstrated that binge eating disorder is by far the most widespread eating problem in America.

What Are Eating Disorders?

Although the current Western obsession with slimness and the glamorous portrayal of emaciated women in the media may contribute to the development of eating disorders, genetic vulnerability, personality, and psychological and environmental factors all play major roles in the emergence of these disorders.

Eating disorders can be recognized by a persistent pattern of unhealthy eating or dieting behavior that can cause health problems and/or emotional and social distress. Eating disorders do not discriminate on the basis of sex, age, or race. They can be found in both sexes and all age groups, across a wide variety of races and ethnic backgrounds, and in countries around the world.

The three officially recognized eating disorders are anorexia nervosa, bulimia nervosa, and eating disorders not otherwise specified (EDNOS). Binge eating disorder is currently classified in the EDNOS category. Although there are formal guidelines that health-care professionals use to diagnose eating disorders, unhealthy eating behaviors exist on a continuum. Even if a person does not meet the formal criteria for an eating disorder, she or he may be experiencing unhealthy eating behaviors that cause substantial distress and may be damaging to both physical and psychological health.

People with anorexia nervosa have a body weight that is below what is normal or expected for their age and height, typically less than 85 percent of expected weight. Even at these very low weights, those with the disorder continue to be fearful of weight gain. Their thoughts and feelings about their size and shape have a profound impact on their sense of self and their self-esteem as well as their relationships. Perplexing to the observer is that they often do not recognize or admit the seriousness of their low weight and deny that it may have any permanent adverse health consequences.

Anorexia nervosa comes in two forms. In the restricting subtype, people maintain their low body weight purely by restricting food intake and sometimes by excessive exercise. Individuals with the binge-eating/purging type also restrict their food intake, but regularly engage in binge eating and/or purging behaviors such as self-induced vomiting or the misuse of laxatives, diuretics, or enemas. The boundaries between the subtypes are fluid, and many people move back and forth between subtypes during the course of their illness. Cases of anorexia nervosa have been described throughout history in many different cultural contexts. Until the 1970s the number of new cases increased but since then has been stable.

People with bulimia nervosa experience binge-eating

episodes marked by eating an unusually large amount of food, usually within a couple of hours, and feeling out of control while doing so. For example, during a binge an individual may feel compelled to eat, and find it extremely difficult if not impossible to stop eating. This is similar to what people experience with binge eating disorder, except those with bulimia nervosa also attempt to undo the consequences of the binge through unhealthy behaviors such as self-induced vomiting, misuse of laxatives, diuretics, severe caloric restriction, or excessive exercising.

There are also two subtypes of bulimia nervosa. The purging type includes those individuals who self-induce vomiting or use laxatives, diuretics, or enemas. The nonpurging type refers to those who compensate through excessive exercising or dietary fasting. Bulimia nervosa is a newer disorder, and between the 1980s and 1990s there was a clear rise in the number of people presenting with this disorder. The number of new cases appears to be stabilizing, with the largest proportion of people presenting for treatment being older adolescents and young adults.

Binge eating disorder is more common among individuals who are overweight or obese, although people of any weight can suffer from the disorder. Other terms for this pattern of eating include compulsive overeating, emotional eating, or food addiction.

Unfortunately, being in the EDNOS category precludes many patients from receiving insurance benefits for the treatment they so desperately need. It also prevents many from seeking help in the first place, as they are frustrated and convinced they'll never have enough money to pay for the treatment.

What do they do instead? Many self-medicate, either with alcohol or over-the-counter drugs or with food—their "drug" of choice. Others ignore the problem, hoping it will go away. And still others deny they have a problem in the first place, figuring that if the medical community doesn't classify binge eating disorder as a "real" eating disorder, then it must not be a concern.

There are many variants of eating disorders that do not fall under these specific headings. In fact, most people with eating disorders have variations, but they need and deserve treatment as much as people suffering from anorexia or bulimia nervosa do.

Regardless of the label, these eating disorders are commonly accompanied by other psychological problems/disorders, including depression, self-mutilation, suicidal behavior, anxiety disorders, obsessive-compulsive disorder, and personality disorders.[4]

A Wake-up Call

The widely reported 2007 Harvard study was the first time in the history of the eating disorders field that binge eating disorder had emerged from the shadows and been "outed," so to speak, as one of psychiatry's most prevalent disorders. Two major news sources broke the story with unprecedented—and in one case, quite personal—national coverage.

The same day the Harvard study came out, *Forbes* magazine published an article that quoted Marc Lerro, executive director of the Eating Disorders Coalition: "This survey is really a wakeup call for the federal government to do more, like counting the number of people who die each year due to an eating disorder, counting the number of people who are struggling with eating disorders, and funding research to determine what is effective in treating eating disorders."[5]

While the *Forbes* story served to vindicate many of us who had been studying eating disorders for years, it finally gave many people who had been suffering from them (undiagnosed) a name to put on their condition. One such person was reporter Jane Brody, who that same February wrote a revealing and very personal story in the *New York Times* telling millions of readers about her struggles with binge eating disorder.

Later, in a more in-depth essay published in *Feed Me!: Writers Dish About Food, Eating, Body Image, and Weight*, Brody revealed the intimate details of what it was like to move from New York to the Midwest, face relationship and job challenges, and suffer from binge eating disorder:

> I never felt like I belonged in Wisconsin, and my feelings of displacement, combined with my dissipating love life, took its toll. Little by little, I turned to food for solace. After all, to me it meant love and acceptance. When I began to gain weight, I went on a diet and lost it, only to regain what I lost when I went off the diet. Still, I wasn't what anyone would call fat when I took a job at the *Minneapolis Tribune,* then one of the nation's top newspapers.
>
> Although Minneapolis provided me with more of a sense of belonging and several friends who remain dear to me to this day, it wasn't long before several problems turned my head to food. My job soon became tedious and not at all what I'd been promised when hired. My boss was a misogynist who did everything possible to thwart my success. My love life was in complete disarray.
>
> Food was about the only thing I could count on for pleasure. And not just any food. Candy bars, ice cream, cookies, crackers, chips, cereal. Note the carbohydrate content—and overall lack of nutrients. I also learned how to drink, in those days almost a necessity if you wanted to be part of the newspaper crowd. (Fortunately, I never got hooked on their smoking habits. Alcohol was bad enough.) I began to gain weight, despite daily physical activity. Naturally, I dieted, trying nearly every diet that had been invented, including the Drinking Man's Diet (which at least allowed me to continue to socialize with my newspaper colleagues). And

naturally, I would soon abandon each diet and regain what I'd lost and then some.

Eventually I discovered that once I started eating, I couldn't stop. So I decided not to eat during the day. I waited until I got off work (usually 10 p.m. or later) and then the gorging began. I soon learned where all the all-night mom-and-pop shops were located and raided them on my way home for that night's consumption.

The pattern of my nightly binges went from sweet to salt and then back to sweet—a half-gallon of ice cream was only the beginning—until sleep overcame me. I often awoke in the morning with partially chewed food still in my mouth. And since I'd never heard of purging (not that I was likely to go that route, since I'd long considered throwing up one of life's most unpleasant events), my binges simply added pounds to my little frame until I weighed a third more than I did in college. When I reached size 14 I stopped buying clothes off the rack and began making my own so I wouldn't have to face the size they were.

And, as you might expect, I became more and more unhappy with my life. One night, after a particularly destructive binge, I became desperate. I was no longer in control of my food, it was controlling me, and I felt I could not go on living that way. I contemplated ending my life as the only way out of my entrapment by food. But I was still rational enough to reach out for help. At my lowest point in the middle of the night I called a psychologist I knew at his home, and his offer to see me first thing in the morning got me through the rest of the night.

If *Forbes* reporting the findings of a Harvard research team to the general reading public helped put a name to a devastating illness, Brody's describing her own experiences with the disorder helped put a face on that term.

As validating as the study was for many of us in the eating disorders community, it also came with sobering news: Less than half of those with a history of an eating disorder said they had ever received treatment. So it appears that we are dealing with a widespread disorder that causes significant distress, but sufferers just aren't getting the help they need, which is why I've written this book: If people can't get into treatment, then *Crave* can bring treatment to them. Together we can tackle this disorder one binge at a time. But to recover from binge eating one must first understand the illness and its cultural and biological causes.

What Constitutes a Binge?

Merriam-Webster defines a binge quite simply as "an act of excessive or compulsive consumption (as of food)." How does science classify a binge? A 1994 determination by the American Psychiatric Association (APA) reported, "To qualify as binge eating, both of the following must be present: Eating an amount of food that is clearly larger than what most persons would eat in a similar situation with the same amount of time, AND a sense that one cannot stop eating or control content or quantity of food intake."[6]

So, there you have it. Two credible sources; two valuable classifications—but still fuzzy and imprecise. One of the challenges of working in this field is helping people define what a binge is.

Most of my patients don't really care how doctors like myself or many other researchers qualify, classify, or even define the word *binge*; the important thing is their experience. I have found that every patient binges differently. They seek out different foods, different quantities of food, different times of day, and different places to binge.

It's important for us to determine not only the origins of why you binge but also how you binge; for that, I must rely on you to be your own diagnostician. Self-reporting can be a challenge for even the most diligent patient. Many people would rather just not deal with the binge episodes, let alone document and relive them. I am asking you to do the uncomfortable opposite and put them under the microscope.

And here's how complicated that can get: For some people, two cookies might feel like a binge. Now, I think you and I will agree that this is a very subjective opinion; two cookies is not really a binge to the world at large, but for someone who really has clamped down on her caloric intake, eating two cookies can make her feel completely out of control. So although the binge isn't objectively large, to that individual the subjective experience involves a large amount of food and feeling out of control.

So what does constitute an objective binge? Two cookies, twelve cookies, twenty-two cookies? Maybe you prefer to measure the extent of a binge by calories. Are five hundred calories a binge? Fifteen hundred calories? Twenty-five hundred calories?

Personally, I don't put a calorie limit on the "what's a binge?" question. Fifteen hundred calories might mean a pint of premium ice cream but a half gallon of a cheaper brand. It could mean half a dozen doughnuts or three bags of pretzels or two dozen chocolate chip cookies.

We've all seen the comic strip character Cathy sitting on her couch, drowning her sorrows in a pint of ice cream, a crumpled bag of cookies, or an open box of doughnuts—or, occasionally, all of the above. Does that make our beloved cartoon heroine a binge eater? Maybe, maybe not. If she stops herself midway through and returns the pint to the freezer or the cookies and doughnuts to the pantry, then no. She's in control and just had a snack. If she feels unable to stop the spoon until the pint is empty, then looks for more, then maybe yes!

But in our supersized world, calories can be very deceiving. Let's base our analysis on typical daily caloric intakes. For a moderately active female between the ages of thirty-one and fifty, the average daily recommended caloric intake is around two thousand calories per day. For the moderately active male in the same age range, it is about twenty-five hundred.[7] So, when we put it in the context of recommended daily intake, to many of us, consuming fifteen hundred calories in one meal sure sounds like a binge (at first), but examine the contents of your average drive-through meal a little more closely and you'll see that it's practically the norm when it comes to fast food. A double cheeseburger with mayonnaise, large fries, and a regular soda or shake could easily constitute fifteen hundred calories—in one sitting—and we're not even talking about the ninety-nine-cent dessert menu. So if we just look at the calories, half of America would seem to be binge eaters; clearly, despite how large the binge-eating population is, this is simply not accurate.

Instead, when considering binge eating, the important parameters are:

1. **That "other people" would view it as an unusually large amount of food**
2. **You feel out of control while eating it**

We talked about the first parameter; now let's address the sense of being out of control. This can refer to a couple of things, and some people experience both, while others identify more with one or the other. The first interpretation is once you start feeling the urge to binge, you seem to have no ability to resist that urge. You feel compelled to binge. In this case, you have no control over the initiation of the binge. The second interpretation is once you start eating—have that first bite of chocolate or first potato chip—you feel like you have no ability to stop eating. In this case, you have no control over the termination of the binge. Either way, you are experiencing a loss of control. Understanding which type (or both) you experience can be important for tailoring your treatment.

What Causes Binge Eating?

Scientists had long believed that eating disorders were primarily triggered by cultural pressures or an individual's psychology. But over the past decade, there's been a real revolution in thinking about the various factors that lead to eating disorders. We now have evidence of the substantial role that genes can play. People who are genetically vulnerable may be more susceptible to cultural pressures and they may turn to food for comfort. That could be the first step on the slippery slope to an eating disorder.

"But why can't you just stop eating?" is the cry heard from loved ones who don't understand why you cannot just will yourself to stop binge eating. So what *is* the reason? The truth is that many people who binge eat may be fighting an uphill battle against their own genes. Genes don't just influence eye color and height; they also play a large role in eating behavior as well—including binge eating.

Experts now realize two truths: First, eating disorders tend to run in families, and second, for many (but not all), binge eating follows closely on the heels of extreme dieting. Knowing that something is genetic doesn't give you a pass to say "forget it, it's out of my control." Rather, this news can literally energize you into understanding the magnitude of the challenge and finding the right tools to transform your behavior.

Societal influences have also contributed to the surge in numbers of binge eaters: No binge eater lives in a vacuum, and few can dispute the powerful hold of today's popular media on our youth- and beauty-oriented culture. No longer bound by our height, our shape, our color, or our weight, those of us who can afford it are urged to create designer bodies. But even though we might look different on the outside, our internal hardwiring remains unchanged and our genes hold fast on the inside. While society, the media, popular culture, and peers pressure us toward vanity-based changes, our DNA remains constant.

From telegenic plastic surgeons to the stars (who become celebrities themselves) to bestselling diet doctors to fashion magazines to movie and rock stars to personal trainers, we are bombarded with images of a better body—at any cost. At the same time, we are offered a glut of over-the-counter remedies bearing the labels QUICK, INSTANT, OVERNIGHT, or IMMEDIATE. If only we gulp a protein shake, gobble a fistful of vitamin supplements or cut out those nasty carbohydrates, the promise is the same: A thinner or younger-looking body leads to a happier life—almost overnight.

So what happens when genes and culture collide? With binge eating disorder, we are in a classic situation of genes loading the gun and environment pulling the trigger. In the chapters that follow, we will explore how your genes might make you more or less vulnerable to those lurking environmental triggers that can send you down the binge-eating pathway. For now, let's examine some of the common triggers that cause binge eating—and how we can best avoid them.

What Are Some Common Triggers?

Everybody says that stress is a common trigger for the binge eater. Well, we can all agree that stress is the devil, but in our current world how can we avoid it? We experience stress about our jobs, money, relationships, retirement, the environment. The trick is to figure out what specific aspect of stress is *your* trigger. Telling someone to decrease the stress in his or her life is not helpful because it is hopelessly nonspecific.

Understanding what patients mean by stress and what kinds of tools they need to deal with it in a healthy way—now *that* can be effective. A former patient of mine, we'll call him "Max," was the classic "nervous eater." He didn't so much have a sweet tooth as a "sweat tooth." He could go days without a doughnut, candy bar, or muffin, but let his boss look at him sideways on Friday and he'd spend the whole weekend reaching for all of the above, as often as possible.

He could spend all morning in the gym and enjoy a healthy lunch of broiled chicken and broccoli with a side of carrot juice to wash it all down, but let him get an overdue bill in the mail or a letter from the IRS and he'd jump in the car and rush to the nearest drive-through or stroll to the closest convenience-store candy aisle.

Max's story is far from uncommon. His buzzword was "upset." His response was to reach for his candy bar or snack cake of choice. For whatever reason, his trigger was emotional and his first instinct was to eat something sweet, gooey, or chocolatey.

If you are an emotional eater the secret to eventual recovery is to figure out what "upset" means to you and how to predict, control, and deal with it in a healthy way, versus reaching for the first candy bar in sight. Stress eating is a huge issue when it comes to binge eating disorder; in fact, stress tops the list of triggers for unhealthy eating behaviors. But to defuse the trigger, you first need to figure out what it means to you—your unique stress-eating profile.

Eating is just the most convenient remedy, a quick fix to relieve your feelings of discomfort with so-called comfort foods. But it doesn't work in the long term. If anything, it makes things worse over time because the habit adds even more stress from having overeaten or gained weight. By trying to make food the issue, by focusing on the food instead of dealing with the stress, the binge eater creates a strategy that is bound to backfire.

Another major trigger for binge eating is deprivation. Skipping breakfast, skipping lunch, and partaking of irregular meals set us up psychologically and biologically for a binge. Psychologically, we're at the mercy of thoughts like, "Well, I saved all of those calories by skipping breakfast, so I've earned an extra dessert tonight." Biologically, our body has gone far too long without nourishment, and when the floodgates open, there's not time for those "I'm full" signals to make their way to your brain and make you to put your fork down.

Part of what we try to teach patients in therapy is that recovery from binge eating disorder does not mean gaining weight. By eating regular meals—especially breakfast and snacks—that are both sensible and healthy, they surprisingly find that they will lose weight more easily. How?

Simple. Let's say that for you, five sensible meals (three meals and two snacks) throughout a routine day can equal twenty-five hundred calories. In contrast, skipping meals and then having a whopping binge at the end of the day to compensate can easily exceed three thousand calories. So even if you think you're saving up, you wind up eating more in the end. While the logic of this calorie math may seem painfully simple, in the heat of the moment, when the urge to binge hits, math is the last thing on your mind.

As you read on, you will learn techniques to identify your binge triggers before they sneak up on you, *and* I will arm you to tackle them in a healthy way. The first thing you need to do is be your own best observer. Open your eyes, spy on yourself, take detailed notes. Become a sleuth about your own behavior. Ask yourself, "What am I eating? What time of day is it? Where am I? What were the triggers for this bout of eating? What's my mood?" The answers can often be startling, particularly when a visible pattern emerges. That telltale pattern often becomes the foundation for a more effective recovery.

Shattering Stereotypes

Many of us share the misconception that all binge eaters are teenage girls "pigging out" in their dorm rooms or closets back home. But both research and clinical experience has shown me that this is far from the case. For instance, a recent patient, I'll call her "Sheila," ballooned up to 220 pounds—gaining over 100 pounds during her pregnancy as a result of binge eating.

Another patient, "Bill," started binge eating after he quit participating in college athletics and gained weight because he was not only binge eating but also exercising less when he was no longer involved in organized sports. These mini case studies will be further fleshed out in the chapters to come and used to exemplify the fact that anyone is at risk for binge eating, including our children and parents.

One fascinating aspect uncovered by the Harvard study was that the number of men suffering from binge eating disorder—some three million of them—was much higher than previously believed. As shockingly large as those numbers are, however, I believe that many men are underreporting. In other words, three million men were found to be *diagnosable* binge eaters, those men who meet the official clinical definition of a binge eater. Many more men are probably suffering from binge eating disorder but neither admitting to it nor getting treatment.

According to the National Eating Disorders Association (NEDA), there are about one million men with anorexia or bulimia and millions more who have some form of disordered eating.[8] The following groups of men have an increased risk for developing eating disorders:

- Athletes, especially those who participate in sports in which leanness equates with performance such as wrestling, rowing, running, ski jumping, cycling, and horse racing

- Athletes whose bulk contributes to performance, such as football players and bodybuilders
- Men with personality traits such as perfectionism and impulsivity, and those who tend to be anxious, obsessive, or depressed
- Obese boys who have been on the receiving end of teasing and who have low self-esteem

Illustrating that no one is immune, in April 2008 Britain's former deputy prime minister John Prescott revealed that he has secretly struggled with bulimia for decades. He described gorging on vast amounts of food and then forcing himself to vomit.

Prescott, who is sixty-nine, stepped down in June and made the admission one month before the publication of his memoirs. He recounted that he first struggled with the eating disorder in the early 1980s when he became a front-line opposition lawmaker. Binge eating became a tactic for coping with stress from overwork. "It became my main pleasure, having access to my comfort food. So what I did was stuff my face with anything around, any old rubbish: burgers, chocolate, crisps, fish and chips, loads of it, 'til I felt sick," he said.[9]

Part of the reason men are reluctant to interpret their pattern of bingeing as an eating disorder is a misconception men and women have about who suffers from the disorder. Don't believe me? Here's a quick test: it's a word association game. When I say *anorexia* or *bulimia*, what is your first mental picture? A teenage girl, right? Odds are you have the same mental picture when you hear the words *eating disorder*. And why wouldn't you? After all, teenage girls—often looking pathetically thin, haggard, wan, and depressed—are the default depiction of eating disorders. We see them staring back at us from book covers, magazine articles, and Web sites. Naturally, our brains link the two: eating disorders = teenage girls.

Although some of the nine million diagnosed binge eaters in the country *are* teenage girls, most are not. Binge eating disor-

der does not discriminate on any dimension—gender, race, ethnicity, sexual orientation, or age. Sisters and brothers, mothers
and grandmothers, baby boomers and midlifers, coaches and
athletes are all potential victims.

With more and more publicity surrounding the dangers of
eating disorders and the abundance of treatment options
available, it might seem "safe" for anyone of any age to report
and seek treatment for an eating disorder. Yet put yourself in
the shoes of a middle-aged businessman going from one drive-
through to another, gorging on twenty-five hundred to three
thousand calories in a single sitting, filled with shame, doubt,
guilt, and confusion. And then try to admit to your friends,
family, wife, co-workers, or even boss that you have what is
perceived as a "teenage girl's" disease. It is vitally important to
eliminate stereotypes that erect barriers to diagnosis and
treatment.

Waxing and Waning:
How Binge Eaters Go Undiagnosed

Another problem with diagnosing binge eating disorder is the
fluctuating nature of the disease itself. Many binge eaters start
having problems with food from a very early age. The pattern is
not necessarily consistent, and snapshots of their life at any
given time might catch them during a period when they are doing relatively well (i.e., not binge eating) or, alternatively, feeling out of control.

From my clinical experience, I generally find binge eaters to
fall into one of three categories:

I. **Slow and steadies:** This type of binge eater claims to
   barely remember when it all started. They might recall
   taking a batch of cookies (or raw cookie dough) up to
   their bedroom as a child and bingeing. Their binge

eating has been a constant companion throughout their lives and doesn't seem to vary with the season or time of life.

2. **Four seasons:** Some people find that their binge eating takes on a seasonal pattern. Just like we have learned that some people tend to suffer more from depression in the fall and winter months (seasonal affective disorder, or SAD), we also see people who manage to keep their binges under control in the spring and summer, but find themselves struggling with them again as the days grow shorter and colder.

3. **Hibernators:** Still others find their binge eating comes and goes—often corresponding to major transitions in their lives (e.g., leaving for college, marrying, divorcing, changing jobs) or biologically complicated events such as pregnancy and menopause. And for many months, or even years, at a time, they truly don't have a problem with binge eating. But their binge eating disorder doesn't go away; it simply goes underground. That's right: Many binge eaters can go weeks, months, or even years without an episode. Then some event happens: the death of a family member or friend, the loss of a job, a move from one town to another, or even something as minor as an insensitive remark from a well-meaning friend or family member, and *bam*, just like that, they return to the familiar binge-eating behavior.

Don't choose a category that you think you fall into yet; we've got a lot more ground to cover, and I don't want you to pigeonhole yourself too soon.

So if a binge eater can be anybody, what does the average person suffering from binge eating disorder look like? Well, that's just it; if a binge eater can *be* anybody, they can also *look like* just about anybody. Some of those you'll read about throughout this book include:

- **Drive-through soccer mom.** Linda, a forty-something mom, spends more time in her minivan than anywhere else. With three children under twelve, she is constantly shuttling them from school to music lessons to sports and back again. With a two-pound bag of M&M's in her glove compartment, she is never more than an arm's length away from a binge. Being stuck in traffic is no obstacle to her satisfying her cravings for chocolate.

- **Sandwich generation dad.** Ronald is trying to save funds to send his children to college but at the same time dealing with medical bills from his parents' hospital stays and retirement home. His Sunday mornings are spent poring over bills with nothing to comfort him but doughnuts and coffee.

- **Adult daughter with "mother" issues.** Lucy's biggest trigger for binge eating seems to be her mother. Whether it's a phone call, a visit, or a memory that makes her roll her eyes and clench her jaw, something about their relationship just sends her straight to the fridge.

- **Busy single parent.** Cheryl is an emergency room nurse and single mom, which means no time for herself—ever. As she runs back and forth between the ER and other areas of the hospital, she can practically hear the vending machines calling her name. The more stressed she becomes, the louder they call. Never taking the time to pack a lunch in the morning, she considers the vending machines her only dining option.

"WILL I EVER BE COVERED?"

Insurance is a huge issue for those suffering from eating disorders; treatment can be long-term and, if you're paying for it out of pocket, extremely expensive! Sufferers from anorexia nervosa and bulimia nervosa, recognized eating disorders, find some relief in insurance coverage. For now, many with binge eating disorder still find that their insurance doesn't pay for treatment.

Binge eating disorder is a nasty syndrome with serious health implications, but there is effective evidence-based treatment available to those who can afford it and access it. Being able to find treatment for binge eating disorder can depend on where you live. Help may be more available in an urban area than in a rural one. Once binge eating disorder gets more name recognition, we hope that it will get adequate and/or comparable research funding and insurance coverage as well. And that means you and millions like you can get the help you so desperately need.

Blurring the Lines:
How to Tell When Overeating Becomes Bingeing

Another aspect of binge eating disorder that makes it so hard to classify is the blurry line between simple overeating—which we all do on occasion, especially during holiday celebrations—and binge eating. Overeating in general means eating more food than your body needs to maintain good health and a healthy weight for your body type. Overeating does not usually make you feel out of control when you overindulge.

Binge eating may involve out-of-control eating, uncomfortable fullness after eating, and eating large amounts of food when not hungry. Feelings of shame, guilt, and embarrassment are prominent among binge eaters. People with binge eating disorder engage in binge eating but do not regularly use unhealthy compensatory weight-control behaviors such as fasting or purging to lose weight.

Research criteria provided by the American Psychiatric Association over a decade ago use the following various guidelines to separate simple overeating from binge eating: Three or more of the following are associated with the binge-eating episodes:

- Eating is notably faster than normal
- Eating occurs until the person is beyond full, to the point of discomfort
- The binge occurs when the person is not physically hungry
- The person chooses to eat alone because the amount of food consumed is embarrassing
- Disgust with oneself, depression, or guilt is present after overeating

Although some or all of these descriptors may apply, one defining feature is that the binge eating causes distress or impairment. Either the binge eater is distressed by the eating episodes or the binge eating begins to interfere with his or her life. Distress is pretty easy to understand, but how can binge eating lead to impairment? If you would rather stay at home with food than spend time with your friends or family, if you lie about your eating and it causes conflict in your relationship, if it interferes with school or work, then your binge eating has led to impairment in important realms of your life.

Although the APA states that binge eating must occur "an average of at least two days per week for six months" in order to meet diagnostic criteria, this is arbitrary: Some people binge eat more often, some less. Regardless of the frequency, binge eating should be taken seriously.

Okay, so we've heard from Merriam-Webster, the APA, and my own opinion about what, specifically, determines whether one is a binge eater. But what about *you*? Does this information help you define your own lingering symptoms and/or classify yourself as a bona fide binge eater?

Many people have, at one time or another, crossed the line between simply "pigging out" and truly binge eating. But when? How often? By how many calories? And, more important, how did they feel about themselves before, during, or afterward? These are all questions to put to yourself if you want to truly know whether you are a binge eater.

The following questions are ones I don't necessarily ask in clinical situations, but in more casual scenarios when I'm helping someone in a nonclinical setting understand the nature of his or her eating. Say a family member, friend, or colleague of mine is concerned about her daughter, her son, her husband— or herself.

I would ask her to guesstimate as to her status as an occasional overeater versus a classic binge eater. For some people it is important to make the distinction, but what these questions really get at is whether you have an unhealthy relationship with food.

- Do I feel compelled to eat when an urge to binge is coming on?
- Have I always had "issues" with food?
- Do I have negative weight associations, i.e., "fat" is "bad" and "thin" is "good"?
- Do I frequently lie about the amount of food I eat?
- Do I often wait until I'm alone to eat?
- Once I start eating do I have difficulty stopping?
- Do I build my day around eating?
- Do I hide secret stashes of food around the house/in the car?
- Do I have feelings of shame, guilt, remorse, or inadequacy after overeating?
- Do I have a list of "bad foods" that I secretly crave?

- Do I often "black out" or "zone out" during overeating, to the point where I barely remember, let alone taste, what I ate?

Binge eating disorder is serious. As we have seen, it is currently affecting millions of men, women, and children in this country. The effects can be devastating. From feelings of guilt and shame to health risks such as insomnia, obesity, type 2 diabetes, and chronic pain, the risks are real. As I stated in the beginning of this chapter, there *is* hope for the future. Almost every month, it seems, new studies emerge supporting the notion that recovery is an attainable goal.

Whether the binge eating belongs to you, your daughter, your husband, or your neighbor, and whether you are experiencing binge eating or simply overeating, the tools in this book can help you repair your relationship with food and with your own body.

In subsequent chapters we will continue to build on the solid foundation we've laid out in chapter 1. If you are one of the one in thirty-five who suffer from binge eating disorder, the information can help you gain control over your eating and keep you from being a slave to your crave.

CHAPTER 2

Weight Loss and Binge Eating

Although one of the national health objectives for the year 2010 is to reduce the prevalence of obesity among adults to less than 15%, current data indicate that the situation is worsening rather than improving.
—THE CENTERS FOR DISEASE CONTROL (CDC)[1]

Tish has spent years battling binge eating disorder; many of those years were spent as a frontline "eating disorder warrior" before the disorder even had a name. Through it all, weight loss has been a critical reason behind Tish's uncontrollable binge eating.

"My father had a lot to say about my weight," explains Tish. "He never liked it when I put on pounds as a young girl, and especially as a growing girl. He once offered to pay me five dollars for every pound I lost as a teenager; kind of the same thing some parents do by paying their kids so many dollars for each A. Right about then I learned the 'value' of being thin; and I never forgot it."

Later, her second husband, whom she is no longer with, took over where her father left off. "I'll never forget when I was pregnant with our son; he [her husband] literally asked me to use the guest bathroom when I showered so that he wouldn't have to watch me 'gain weight,' even though this was baby weight!"

Such disparaging remarks can lead to negative self-talk, and often to a horrible body image; not surprisingly, Tish had both—for quite some time. Since then, she has ridden the binge eating disorder roller coaster, largely avoiding treatment by being what we identified in the first chapter as a hibernator. Her binge-eating behavior would come and go; sometimes she would shut it off by sheer force of will.

When she was pregnant with her daughter, for instance, she quit binge eating altogether and allowed herself to feel comfortable gaining a considerable amount of pregnancy weight. She did the same thing with her next baby a few years later; she knew the physical effects of binge eating were dangerous and didn't want it to affect either child.

Tish also went through bouts of bulimia nervosa—when her binge eating was coupled with purging behaviors. It's not uncommon for an eating disorder to have many "faces" during the course of a person's life. In Tish's case, to lose the pregnancy weight, she resorted to extreme behaviors: binge eating and purging, then, instead of purging, bingeing on excessive exercise to counteract the increased caloric intake.

She tells of many days in which she would exercise vigorously in the morning, fit in as much exercise on her work breaks as possible (climbing the stairs, parking in the remotest space in the parking lot so that she could walk farther), and then go to an exercise class in the evening. Still, hours later, she'd feel as if she had not burned off enough calories to counter her binges, so she'd exercise on her own, after class, as well—often late into the night on an exercise bike she kept in the house for just such occasions.

She has suffered endless bouts of anxiety, fear, doubt, insecurity, and depression, as well as physical injuries. Even now she is recovering from her third rotator cuff surgery, a condition she blames in part on her excessive exercising over the years or, as she calls it, "overdoing it even after I'd overdone it!"

Tish's story illustrates the twin dangers that affect so many binge eaters: having an eating disorder and being overweight. Since binge eating disorder does *not* involve purging, the weight issue can become particularly daunting; life becomes a balancing act where the thousands of calories consumed during a binge have to go somewhere. Either they pile on as extra weight, or life becomes an endless cycle of skipped meals and binges. Neither is a recipe for good health.

Too often the escalating weight and out-of-control binges lead to a sense of hopelessness. The person stops caring and fears that his or her overeating and weight are "lost causes." Where do those feelings of despair and powerlessness send the binge eater? More often than not, right back to the fridge, the convenience store, or the drive-through window.

This battle becomes persistent, even ingrained, in the life of the classic binge eater. Talking to Tish, I can see not only the past pain of old wounds but also the fresh anxiety and self-doubt that accompany talking about them. Although she's been "out of the woods" with the disorder for some time now, we both know that recovery can be an ongoing process. I think one of the most frustrating parts of recovery for many people with this disorder is the lingering effects that seem to dog them throughout their lives.

Like Tish, they can often feel like "damaged goods" for years after beginning their recovery. That is why it is so important to get this information out there—to you, to your family members, to your friends, to *their* family members and friends—so that faster diagnoses and shorter recovery times can become the norm, not the exception.

Each eating disorder is different. Bulimia nervosa is often called the "invisible" eating disorder because you can't tell by looking at someone's body that she or he has it—unlike anorexia nervosa, where people who have it are so painfully thin. Binge eating disorder, in most cases, is also visible because many binge eaters do struggle with their weight, although some do not become overweight.

It's difficult today to pick up a newspaper or magazine without being reminded that being overweight takes a toll on your health, but you need to look at that information in a way that pertains to you and, ultimately, your own health: How dangerous is being overweight? How will it affect me? My children? My friends and family? What part of my body, even my mind, can being overweight damage? It's important for us to know how being overweight affects our bodies and our minds.

First, let's clarify terminology. The two terms you will most often hear are *overweight* or *obese*. The medical world uses a metric called body mass index (BMI) in order to classify people's weight while accounting for their height. Regular BMI measurements work for adults, but special care has to be taken when calculating BMI for children and adolescents, where it is best to use a measure of BMI percentile, which also takes their age and gender into account.

According to the World Health Organization (WHO), a healthy BMI range is between 18.5 and 24.9 kg/m^2. To calculate your BMI, either weigh yourself in kilograms (kg) and divide that by your height in meters squared (m^2) or go to your computer and access one of the U.S. government Web sites that provides BMI calculators for you to determine your BMI. (The Centers for Disease Control, at www.cdc.gov, has addressed the age issue by having both adult and child and teen BMI calculators.)

The Centers for Disease Control uses BMI to classify normal adult weight and what's above and below normal:[2]

BMI	WEIGHT STATUS
Below 18.5	Underweight
18.5–24.9	Normal
25.0–29.9	Overweight
30.0 and above	Obese

By and large, BMI is a widely accepted measurement for size. It holds for men and women and across the adult age span. There are ongoing debates about whether special charts are required for people of different racial and ethnic backgrounds. But regardless, the guidelines are worthy of attention.

Most of what we know about the ill-effects of weight comes from studies of obese individuals, those with BMI numbers over 30. Although there is also evidence of negative health consequences in the overweight range, the higher the BMI, the greater the health risks.

To that end, research across a variety of disciplines indicates that obesity endangers a wide array of bodily systems. From hypertension to a greater risk of contracting type 2 diabetes, from coronary heart disease to stroke to osteoarthritis and even to cancer, it would seem there are very few areas of one's life that *don't* become compromised by being significantly overweight.

Later in this chapter we will discuss these health risks in more detail, but for now it is important to at least recognize them in the broad sense and then discuss the subject that is always lurking in the shadows when it comes to any eating disorder, particularly binge eating disorder: weight loss.

If being overweight has its inherent risks, then we need to discuss healthy ways of controlling weight that will not catapult you into other forms of eating disorders (such as we saw with Tish), which naturally carry with them their own health risks. Ultimately, you are seeking the holy grail of moderation, being neither too extremely thin nor too grossly overweight. Although this sounds simple, for people who are used to extremes, moderation can be hard to grasp. My job is to help you find peace in moderation without feeling deprived or defenseless.

Healthy weight loss has to be a gradual process. You didn't gain all of the weight in one week, so why should you think you can lose it in seven days on the latest fad diet? Just like your struggle with your weight has been lifelong or at least years long, that's the same type of timeline you need to think about when it comes to controlling your weight. I have never understood why we are so gullible as to believe that we can quickly fix things that have taken so long to develop.

Many women think they will get their prepregnancy body back within weeks after having a baby (and the Hollywood "yummie mummies" do nothing to dispel that myth). It took you nine months to develop that special healthy incubator for your baby, and you have to give your body at least nine months (and usually more) to get back to where you were before you became pregnant. And during that time it is more important to focus on nurturing your young baby than on achieving a svelte, ideal figure.

Speedy diets are a sham and a scam. They are biologically impossible and are developed by people who know nothing about the biology of weight loss. And when you are lured into buying magazines and books offering quick-fix promises, you are also being robbed of your hard-earned money.

You *will* drop a few pounds—in the short run—when you go on these diets, but that is nothing but water weight. What we're talking about in terms of a permanent solution is an extreme eating makeover, real long-term behavior changes that you embrace and that become your toolbox for success for the rest of your life.

Long-term behavioral weight control programs (the type we use in our program at UNC) usually result in a weight loss of one to two pounds per week, depending on several factors (e.g., initial body weight, adhering to the lifestyle change). Some weeks you lose more, some weeks you lose less, and some weeks you maintain your current weight; regardless, slow and steady wins the race.

What are the ingredients for success? We know who succeeds at losing weight and keeping it off and what tools they use to succeed. Research shows that participants who lose weight and maintain their weight loss engage in specific behaviors including: regular weighing, keeping a diary, healthy and balanced eating, physical activity of over sixty minutes

---

DESPERATE MEASURES: A SURVEY IN *SELF* MAGAZINE

In 2008 the University of North Carolina at Chapel Hill in collaboration with *Self* magazine conducted an online survey of 4,023 women between the ages of twenty-five and forty-five. The results were astonishing. First, the survey found that unhealthy eating behaviors cut across racial and ethnic lines and were not limited to any one group. Women who identified their ethnic background as Hispanic or Latina, white, black or African American, and Asian were all represented among the women who reported these behaviors. The survey also found an unexpectedly high number of women who engage in unhealthy purging activities. More than 31 percent of the women surveyed reported that in an attempt to lose weight they had induced vomiting or had taken laxatives, diuretics, or diet pills at some point in their lives. Among these women, more than 50 percent engaged in purging activities at least a few times a week and many did so every day. Other findings reported in the survey are as follows:

- 75 percent of women report unhealthy eating behaviors or symptoms consistent with eating disorders; so three out of four have an unhealthy relationship with food or their bodies

per day, modifying behaviors, and maintaining contact with a weight-loss provider.

Physical and psychological risks go hand in hand with the dual problem of binge eating and being overweight. From pain, chronic fatigue, and insomnia to depression and anxiety, binge eating disorder leads to a decreased quality of health and diminished quality of life.

- 67 percent of women (excluding those with actual eating disorders) are trying to lose weight
- 53 percent of dieters are already at a healthy weight and are still trying to lose weight
- 39 percent of women say concerns about what they eat or weigh interfere with their happiness
- 37 percent regularly skip meals to try to lose weight
- 27 percent would be "extremely upset" if they gained just five pounds
- 26 percent cut out entire food groups
- 16 percent have dieted on a thousand calories a day or fewer
- 13 percent smoke to lose weight
- 12 percent often eat when they're not hungry; 49 percent sometimes do

Sadly, these revelations appear to be desperate yet ineffective attempts to stem the rising tide of obesity. In the accompanying article in *Self* entitled "The Disorder Next Door" by Tula Karras,[3] we encouraged women to even out their behavior by adopting a moderate approach to eating, separating mood from food, eliminating extreme thinking, eating breakfast, and finding realistic body role models.

The Health Risks of Obesity

Smoking, obesity, poverty—a choice no one wants to make. But what is the relative impact of these conditions on the population?

According to the RAND Corporation, obesity is widely recognized as a health risk. The negative effects of obesity, smoking, heavy drinking, and poverty have been well documented. But until now, no one has compared them. Is one problem worse than another? Or are they all equally risky? Two RAND researchers, health economist Roland Sturm and psychiatrist Kenneth Wells, examined the comparative effects of obesity, smoking, heavy drinking, and poverty on chronic health conditions and health expenditures. Their finding: Obesity is the most serious problem. It is linked to a major increase in chronic health conditions and significantly higher health expenditures. And it affects more people than smoking, heavy drinking, or poverty.[4]

My fellow researchers and I grapple with the fact that being overweight or obese and having an eating disorder are not taken seriously—sometimes even within the academic and medical communities where people often believe that with a little will power or restraint and self-control "these people" should be able to get a grip and solve their problems.

Well, it's just not that simple—or we wouldn't be bombarded by these epidemics. Truth be told, most doctors don't have a clue when it comes to giving their patients advice about weight loss or eating disorders. They might be able to say "you need to lose weight" or "you have to stop binge eating," but when it comes to how, their toolbox is often empty—leaving their patients holding the bag.

On the other hand, other serious medical conditions with equally serious complications get all the press, the funding, and the (media) attention. Nicotine is addictive; smokers need help. Alcoholism is a disease; alcoholics need help. Poverty is a

socioeconomic blight and its sufferers require federal assistance. But an eating disorder? Carrying around thirty or forty
extra pounds? "Come on, people, read a diet book and help
yourselves!" seems to be the general consensus.

It seems as if the popular media are not only hypersensitive
to weight, but realize our insecurities about the issue and
profit from them with tantalizing, sensational headlines aimed
squarely at our weaknesses. When you check out of the grocery
store, you don't see magazine headlines that say STOP DRINKING
IN 7 DAYS WITH THE NEW SEAWEED TREATMENT or THE HOLLYWOOD SECRET
TO STAMPING OUT THOSE CANCER STICKS! In other words, we don't
trivialize these other complex, serious health issues with trite
solutions. Why should eating disorders be any different?

Sadly, this pull-yourself-up-by-the-bootstraps sentiment is
often shared by patients' families, friends, and even significant others, making treatment all the more challenging—and
sometimes unsuccessful. I'm not saying you shouldn't grab
your bootstraps—recovery is all about personal accountability—
but I am acknowledging that you need help and direction in
doing so.

While society continues to misunderstand the environmental and genetic causes of obesity and eating disorders, necessary funding for treatment, medical, and outreach programs
suffers. Meanwhile, the dangers of obesity continue to be felt
by those in need.

Let's look at some other definitions of *overweight* and *obesity*.
According to the American Heart Association, "Obesity is defined simply as too much body fat. Your body is made up of water, fat, protein, carbohydrates, and various vitamins and
minerals. If you have too much fat—especially in your waist
area—you're at higher risk for health problems, including high
blood pressure, high blood cholesterol, diabetes, heart disease
and stroke. Obesity is now recognized as a major risk factor for
coronary heart disease, which can lead to heart attack."[5]

This waist area issue is important. We have two general body types: apples and pears (although there are many variations on those themes). In general, it is when your weight is carried around your middle—creating the "apple" shape—that the health risks are greatest. If you are someone who carries your weight in your hips and below—the "pear" shape—the health risk aren't as great.

We have heard about the health risks of obesity countless times. So many, perhaps, that we have become immune to the warnings. It's a little like the boy who cried wolf: We finally ignore the symptoms until it's too late for rescue. It's as if we can say "hypertension," "high cholesterol" and "type 2 diabetes" until we are blue in the face, and people's eyes start to glaze over. Maybe that's because the perception is that there are medications that can be taken to counteract those very serious conditions. Are you overweight and have high cholesterol but still want a triple cheeseburger? Well, then just pop a statin pill and have your cheeseburger and eat it, too!

But some new research is beginning to reveal obesity-associated health consequences—like depression, dementia, and even cancer—for which there aren't convenient medications. New research from a report by the Group Health Center for Health Studies establishes a "clear link between obesity and depression, anxiety" and other mood disorders.

The Group Health study was first published in the July 2006 *Archives of General Psychiatry*. "People who are overweight or obese are more likely to have anxiety or depression problems. They're really stigmatized," said Dr. Gregory Simon, a psychiatrist and researcher at Group Health. "There had been previous research saying there appeared to be a link between obesity and depression—the results weren't surprising—but this study made it clearer."[6]

Further evidence goes beyond mere depression to state that being overweight or obese may contribute to dementia later in life. According to the Associated Press, the most convincing research so far suggests that being fat in your forties might raise your risk of developing dementia later in life.[7] In a study that followed more than ten thousand Californians for almost thirty years, researchers found that the fatter people were, the greater their risk for Alzheimer's disease or other forms of dementia. Conducted by the Kaiser Permanente Medical Foundation, the California study was funded by the National Institutes of Health (NIH) and first reported in the *British Medical Journal*.[8]

Equally chilling is new research that indicates a more direct link between obesity and breast cancer. Studying the possible relation between weight gain and breast cancer among 44,161 postmenopausal women, a team of American Cancer Society researchers first reported the link between what they call "lifetime weight gain" and cancer in the July 1, 2006, issue of *Cancer*.

According to the study, "Women with over 60 pounds of adult weight gain were nearly two times as likely as women with 20 pounds or less of adult weight gain to develop one form of breast cancer. Weight gain was associated with increased risk for all types, stages, and grades of breast cancer, particularly advanced cases."[9]

This lifetime weight gain seems to be a critical factor, particularly in women after menopause. Says the National Cancer Institute, "Scientists estimate that about 11,000 to 18,000 deaths per year from breast cancer in U.S. women over age 50 might be avoided if women could maintain a BMI under 25 throughout their adult lives."[10]

But it's not just the "freshman fifteen," the middle-aged spread, the baby boomer bellies, or the sedentary habits of our seniors that cause real and grave health concerns for those struggling with their weight or even obesity. If trends continue for our overweight younger adults, their futures are not only looking grimmer by the second, but may also be shorter as a result of their eating and exercise habits.

Can obesity affect our lifespan? According to new research, more than might have previously been suspected. As first reported in the March 17, 2005, issue of the *New England Journal of Medicine*, a team of scientists supported in part by the National Institute on Aging (NIA) found that, over the next few decades, "life expectancy for the average American could decline by as much as 5 years unless aggressive efforts are made to slow rising rates of obesity."[11]

S. Jay Olshansky, Ph.D., of the University of Illinois at Chicago, who reported the study's findings along with Leonard Hayflick, Ph.D., of the University of California, San Francisco, Robert N. Butler, M.D., of the International Longevity Center in New York, and others explain, "Looking out the window, we see a threatening storm—obesity—that will, if unchecked, have a negative effect on life expectancy."

Adds Olshansky, "Unless effective population-level interventions to reduce obesity are developed, the steady rise in life expectancy observed in the modern era may soon come to an end and the youth of today may, on average, live less healthy and possibly even shorter lives than their parents." This means, that for the first time in history, our children may have shorter lifespans than we do.

Finally, based on a study published in the journal *Circulation*, the Associated Press reports that "Excess body fat in teens—even those who are not overweight—seems to be linked to less elastic blood vessels, a condition that can mean future cardiovascular disease, researchers say in a new study. The findings underscore the dangers of the obesity epidemic, even in youngsters. An estimated 30 percent of schoolchildren are believed to be overweight."[12]

I could go on and on, but the research is clear: There are very real dangers of carrying excess body weight around. The point of reviewing these facts is not scare mongering, but just making you aware of the real dangers associated with obesity. In later chapters I will give you specific ways to curb the behaviors that lead to these conditions. For now, though, let's examine the dangers of binge eating disorder when combined with being overweight.

The Dangers of Binge Eating Disorder

As Tish's story—and a few thousand more I could relate—indicates, binge eating disorder takes its toll on the body, mind, and eventually even the soul. Witness her aches and pains, recent surgery, damaged "insides," and general frustration with the harm that's been done to her body over the years.

To look at Tish, you would think this vibrant, intelligent professional woman had the world by the tail. And increasingly she does. But dig deeper, start talking about binge eating disorder, and her "war" stories really do give her the look and feel of a battle-scarred veteran. And while the research done on obesity is staggering, the number of studies done on eating disorders continue to underwhelm.

Still, from the research we *have* gathered over the last few decades, binge eating disorder confers additional physical and psychological problems beyond all of those caused by being overweight. Sometimes it is hard to tease out the effects of obesity from the effects of binge eating disorder, but in some large studies, we have been able to isolate specific effects of binge eating itself.

In a series of studies conducted in the United States and Norway, the risks associated with being overweight were separated out from those associated with binge eating. The U.S. study compared obese women with binge eating disorder to obese women who had no histories of binge eating. The obese women who also reported binge eating said they were more dissatisfied with their health and had higher rates of major medical disorders than obese women who didn't binge eat. The women who were obese and binged also had more depression, anxiety, and alcohol dependence.

In the Norwegian study of 8,045 twins, in women, once you removed the effect of BMI on their health, binge eating was independently associated with insomnia. In men, the story was even more dramatic, with binge eating being independently

associated with anxiety; smoking; alcohol use; use of pain medication; neck and shoulder, lower back, and chronic muscular
pain; and impairment due to physical and mental health. These
studies really highlighted the fact that binge eating is a red flag
for both medical and mental health problems.

There are considerable physical and emotional costs associated with binge eating. That is exactly why what we are trying
to do in the field of eating disorders is so much harder than
simply treating a disease. Few disorders are as complex and
personal as binge eating disorder, where the shame of admitting the problem coupled with the unwillingness of patients
to seek treatment—or, if they do seek treatment, insurance
companies' failure to provide coverage—creates a "perfect
storm" of denial, dismay, and disappointment.

Binge eaters can be particular about what they eat; their cravings are often highly specific and based on a variety of factors:
ability to comfort, taste, and even the location of the food source
(e.g., pantry, convenience store, fast-food restaurant, etc.) That
is not to say, however, that binges are particularly healthy. In fact
binge eaters often prefer quick, easy, and "fast" foods that are
naturally high in fats and carbohydrates. Sacrificing other nutrients such as protein or those found in fruits and vegetables can
lead to a variety of medical complications due to poor nutrition.
These include such physical conditions as high blood pressure,
high cholesterol, and heart disease and such emotional consequences as stress, depression, and anxiety.

Although we have mortality estimates for anorexia and bulimia nervosa, we do not know whether binge eating disorder
increases mortality risk. But why wait for those statistics before
changing your behavior? Even the premature deaths secondary
to hypertension, diabetes, and cancer should be enough to
convince you to change your behavior now.

FEDERAL FUNDING IN THE UNITED STATES

Eating-disorder research has been hampered by very low federal funding levels (approximately $28 million per year), compared to funding for other conditions:

- Alcoholism receives eighteen times more funding ($505 million)
- Schizophrenia receives thirteen times more funding ($352 million)
- Depression receives twelve times more funding ($328 million)
- Food safety receives twelve times more funding ($333 million)
- Sleep disorders receive seven times more funding ($187 million)
- ADHD receives four times more funding ($105 million)

Around the world, research funding for eating disorders does not match funding for comparable conditions.[13]

Double Trouble

And now we find ourselves at a perilous juncture indeed, where the dangers of being overweight clash with the risks of binge eating disorder. According to the National Institute of Mental Health, "Research at NIMH and elsewhere has shown that individuals with binge eating disorder have high rates of co-occurring psychiatric illnesses—especially depression. Obese people with binge eating disorder often have coexisting psychological illnesses including anxiety, depression, and personality disorders."[14]

Tish is a tough cookie; she solved her own issues with binge eating through self-help and sought psychiatric care only *after* her binge eating disorder was already in remission. Luis was another story. He came to our program because he was a salesperson and on the road most of the time. His biggest challenge was his depression.

When he stayed on his medication and his mood was stable, he could manage the cravings and avoid the binges. But if he started skipping his meds and his mood started to slip, he lost all motivation to eat healthfully. Self-defeating thoughts like "Why should I even try? I'm just going to blow it again anyhow" would sneak into his head and he would find himself in a hotel room somewhere surrounded by pizza boxes and Chinese take-out. Keeping an eye—and a handle—on his mood was the top priority in managing his binge eating.

But it was an uphill battle; changes don't happen overnight, and since Luis was already a middle-aged professional who had been having these feelings—and binges—off and on for most of his life, there were serious health complications to consider.

Luis didn't just feel stressed because of his disorder; stress often caused the binges. This combination, if he hadn't caught it in time, could have pushed his blood pressure into the danger zone and marked him as a serious candidate for heart disease. Likewise, his food choices when on the road or during a binge were often of the quick, fast, junk-, and take-out food variety, which didn't help the problem.

What I find so disturbing about Luis's case, however, is how all of the risks and danger signals discussed in the previous two sections were there, flying under the radar because Luis managed to function so well in society. Yet there in the privacy of his hotel room on the road, far away from family and friends, he removed the mask that disguised so much of his unhealthy behavior. For many years, it was almost a Jekyll and Hyde existence.

To look at Luis—or Tish or so many other people with binge

eating disorder—you wouldn't notice anything wrong on the surface. He's successful in his job and managing his family okay; maybe he's slightly overweight, enough for a doctor's warning, but nothing extreme. The pain of struggling with binge eating is hidden, not only from doctors but from colleagues and loved ones as well.

With binge eating disorder, sufferers often go unnoticed, letting the dangers to their health and well-being go unchecked while the disorder smolders. Meanwhile, they become ticking time bombs, waiting to explode with a variety of full-blown symptoms that could not only derail their health but also their recovery from the disorder.

That is why recognizing the signs of the disorder and addressing them promptly are so important to a successful treatment program. Unfortunately, binge eaters can be expert at hiding their behavior.

Consider the college co-ed secretly eating in her dorm room when her roommate's in class, the housewife gorging while her husband's at work and her children are at school, the businessperson traveling a few days out of every week, or the long-distance trucker with a veritable smorgasbord of truck stops, drive-throughs, and greasy spoons along his or her route.

If you think you are suffering from this disorder, you must be vigilant about recognizing the warning signs and confronting the behavior honestly—and quickly. If you suspect someone you know or love has this disorder, you must be equally vigilant and just as vocal. As we have seen, you risk more than just getting high blood pressure or gallstones; the crossroads of obesity and binge eating disorder could influence whether you will be around to see your grandchildren and healthy enough to play with them.

Triggers and Motivators

In the previous chapter we discussed some of the emotional "triggers" that poke holes in your resolve to eat regular, healthful meals and lead to out-of-control binges. Now let's talk about what they have to do with how you eat and why they may cause many people with binge eating disorder to become overweight or even obese.

A trigger is any cue, either in the environment or inside your head or your body, that leads you to unhealthy eating or sedentary behaviors. For example, you go clothes shopping in the mall. You get disgusted after trying on twenty things and you say to yourself, "Everything makes me look fat!" You exit the department store right into the food court. You find your comfort in Cinnabon. Clothes shopping is the environmental trigger and the food court was there to answer the call.

An example of an internal trigger might go something like this: You have a fight with your husband. You're angry but can't express your anger directly. You are frowning and clenching your jaw all day and replaying the tape of the fight over and over in your head. That horrible sinking angry feeling is a mood trigger that sends you straight to the pantry. Recognizing your own personal triggers is the first step in conquering your binge eating disorder and getting your weight back under control.

Food is a very powerful short-term fix, and at the moment when you're feeling down or anxious, it gives you an immediate boost or comforts you. What you remember is the relief, but what you *don't* remember is the crash afterward. Because after you do the eating, not only do you feel bad because you didn't fit into the clothes, or because you didn't stick up for yourself in the fight, but you also feel bad about bingeing. What our brains remember isn't the crash; it's the rapid comfort provided by the food court or the moment of relief in the pantry.

Now that we've identified some of the more common triggers preceding a binge, let's go farther upstream and look at several motivators that can both precede a binge and hopefully sustain a recovery from binge eating disorder.

One of the aspects of treatment that I see people struggling with the most is motivation for physical activity. Reaching and maintaining a healthy weight during treatment for binge eating disorder can be tricky business because now more than ever eating healthful foods on a regular basis and making physical activity a high priority will help with your moods, with decreasing stress, and with filling up time that used to be dedicated to binge eating.

I'm not talking about becoming a gym rat. Again, we're talking about an activity makeover—changing the way you look at the world and approach devices of convenience. This means making use of the stairs instead of the elevator, parking farther away from the store entrance, standing up to change channels on the TV set instead of using the remote. If you add up all the energy you *don't* expend by using modern technological devices, it would total about six pounds a year. I'm not saying you should go down to the stream to wash your clothes by hand, but be mindful of increasing your activity.

In later chapters I'll discuss in greater detail strategies for dealing with triggers and for increasing your physical activity. I can help you do both in ways that are rewarding and long-lasting. But in this early awareness phase it's important to recognize that contemporary societal norms can actually *make it harder* to eat right and exercise.

Reaching plateaus during weight loss is another common stumbling block and you should plan for it. When the dreaded plateau does come, I say "Embrace the Plateau!" Rather than becoming discouraged by your weight loss coming to a screeching halt, you might want to examine that thought process and replace it with a healthier one such as "I've done a great job losing X number of pounds and my body is adjusting to the new weight."

And instead of thinking of weight loss in terms of large, twenty-five-pound increments, it's better to think smaller, in increments of, say, five pounds and plan for the next plateau. With each plateau you reach, it's important to congratulate yourself for the success you've had, spend some time allowing your body and mind to adjust to the plateau, and get ready to increase your activity, which is the best way out of a plateau.

Three Secrets for Demystifying Weight Loss/Gain

My involvement with eating disorders might have begun officially when I was asked to write a chapter comparing brain-

---

HIGH FASHION

Three runway model deaths recently met with an anemic response from the Council of Fashion Designers of America. The fashion world is a push-me-pull-you between starvation and indulgence. With anorexia nervosa on one hand and binge eating and drug and alcohol use on the other, young models around the world are at severe risk. Cases in point:

- In November of 2006, Brazilian model Ana Carolina Reston died; she weighed less than ninety pounds.
- Model Luisel Ramos, twenty-two, died of heart failure in August 2006 during a fashion show at a Montevideo hotel.
- In February of 2007 Eliana Ramos, Luisel's sister—also a model—died in Uruguay; she was only eighteen. Her death was listed as "heart attack," which local medical officials believed to be related to malnutrition.

Sociocultural pressures go both ways—they push us to extremes of emaciation as well as extremes of obesity. We have to exert effort to maintain our position in the healthy middle.

---

wave patterns during sleep in patients suffering from anorexia nervosa and depression and I became fascinated with the disorder. But the experience was both professional and personal: Back in the 1970s I was a figure skater and this assignment gave me a context for problems that many of my fellow figure skaters faced.

While competitive skaters are very aware of their body image and, much like wrestlers competing to stay in a certain weight class or jockeys eager to stay lean and light, must always be watching their weight, it turns out that some of my teammates had bigger problems. In fact I had friends who had trouble with what I later found out was bulimia, but back in the seventies, there was no name for it and, certainly, no treatment available. Suddenly the personal became professional for me, and in a way I've never looked back.

Resisting weight gain and ensuring weight loss or maintenance can be done in healthy ways, as you will discover in later chapters of this book. But here are a few general rules to follow:

1. **First things first:** The most important thing is to make sure you eat breakfast, and I don't mean a cup of coffee while running from your house to the car. People who skip breakfast weigh more and are more likely to binge during the evening hours.

2. **Good and good for you:** Increase your consumption of complex carbohydrates throughout the day. Focus on whole grains, fruits, and vegetables. Complex carbohydrates can help stop cravings.

3. **Combat the crave:** Many people think that a craving will only get stronger and stronger, but the natural pattern of a craving is like a cresting wave: It gets stronger, then comes back down. You have to develop strategies to get over the crest of the wave without succumbing to

a binge; healthy snacks such as a piece of fruit and a glass of water help you do just that.

For those with binge eating disorder, trying to lose (or at least maintain) weight to counter the risks and dangers of obesity is tied to long-closeted weight issues, making the process difficult and even frightening. Taking steps toward major behavior changes can seem daunting, but as you shall soon see, when you take the time, have the patience, and give yourself the permission to solve these issues, your treatment and recovery will benefit.

CHAPTER 3

Be Comfortable in Your Own Genes

Like the alcoholic who loses control after the first drink, these people [binge eaters] can't stop at just one cookie.

—Dr. James I. Hudson of Harvard's
McLean Hospital

Back in the 1980s, when I was training in psychology, I had a supervisor who wouldn't even let me mention the word *biology* to those I was counseling on eating disorders. The approach to treatment was very psychodynamic, with no focus on the symptoms and no focus on genetics, for sure. Instead, we explored topics such as family enmeshment, fears of sexual maturation, and fears of oral impregnation!

Even though the patients spent countless hours exploring these topics in psychotherapy, they were still binge eating and purging, or starving themselves to death. It seemed there had to be a better way—and a quicker one—to get them healthy. As my patients told me stories about their families, one of the themes that resonated was how many other of their family members seemed to have issues with food and weight. It seemed as if these traits might actually be running in families. Despite not being able to use the *b* word (biology) or the *g* word (genetics), I began to wonder quietly whether these behaviors might have genetic components. Midway through my career, I retrained in psychiatric genetics with the hope of gaining new tools to unlock the mysteries of why people really behave the way they do.

Now, I am amazed at the meteoric increase over just the past ten years in the research worldwide (some my own) that has confirmed and extended discoveries about the link between genes and eating disorders such as binge eating disorder. And I'm so moved when I see the heavy load of guilt lift from the shoulders of people like Kathy, a patient from Kissimmee, Florida, as she learns that it's not just about willpower or moral weakness but also about the way her genes and her biology play a role in her unhealthy eating behaviors. She finds solace in the National Eating Disorders Association slogan "Be Comfortable in Your Own Genes."

Kathy is a forty-year-old mother of four whose hectic schedule mirrors that of many working mothers. She is continually ferrying her older boys, age thirteen and nine, and her daughter, eleven, around in her minivan to their after-school activities, or collecting her two-year-old son from day care. She calls her husband, Curtis, a sales manager for a computer supplier, a "great guy," but he works sixty-hour weeks, so the shuttle burden falls on her.

"Most of the time I feel like I'm running a taxi service," she says.

At 5 feet 4 inches and 220 pounds, Kathy sees herself as a "fat lady." She blames her eating habits on her frantic lifestyle. "I'm in the car so much that I spend too much time in the drive-through." She'll grab a drive-through snack on her way to pick up the two-year-old, or hit another fast-food spot for dinner on her way to pick up one of her other kids after a piano lesson or tae kwon do.

Once she gets to the drive-through window, her choices sometimes include not one but three orders of fries with a Diet Coke.

"Why can't you just stop eating?" her slim sister Barbara, who is five years older than Kathy, asks. The answer is not a simple one, because Kathy is a classic out-of-control binge eater. She feels helpless in the face of her appetite, which tends to overtake her when she is most stressed.

The truth is that some people like Kathy who binge eat are fighting an uphill battle against their genes. Rather than simply blaming her out-of-control eating on a stressed-out family life, Kathy first needs to understand how her hardwiring sets her up for an eating disorder. She and her sister (along with her husband and the rest of her family) need to understand the internal programming that puts her at risk, and Kathy must abandon the self-hatred that results from other people's judgment that overeating is an issue of will power alone.

The connection between genes and eating has given us a completely new perspective on our treatment of binge eaters. Even though genes load the gun, choice still plays a role in how often the gun fires—and how damaging the binge becomes. Genes don't act alone in complex behaviors like binge eating. A combination of genes and environment is involved in the decision to pull into the drive-through and choose a salad over a burger, or keep driving home for healthier options. But genes *can* make it harder to make the healthy choice.

The Genetic Link Behind Eating Disorders

Current studies seem to conclude that your hardwiring determines how vulnerable you are to the pernicious behaviors encouraged by the food, fashion, and entertainment industries. Whether the pressure comes from the fashion industry's emphasis on exaggerated thinness or television makeover shows that promise that you, too, can achieve perfection, the extreme dieting that may result can boomerang until your body finally gives in and screams "Feed me!"

While another woman with a different genetic profile might be able to diet and then return to reasonable eating, the physical and psychological deprivation that follows an extreme diet can set off an uncontrollable binge in a woman genetically inclined to binge eating disorder. Let us take a moment here to examine just how our genetic makeup can make it seem like we're literally hardwired to binge.

Before birth, each of us gets a set of chromosomes with genes that influence everything from hair texture to skin color to the risk for certain diseases and disorders. In the past ten years or so, a rash of scientific studies has begun to make it clear that eating disorders such as anorexia and bulimia nervosa run in families. Other studies have shown that obesity is even more closely linked within families.

But only recently have studies comparing families and twins revealed that binge eating disorder can also be an inherited trait passed along from parents to children. As with all genetically influenced disorders, binge eating disorder does not get passed along to every sibling. Unlike single-gene diseases such as Huntington's (if you have the gene, you get the disease), syndromes like binge eating disorder are influenced by many genes and many environmental factors. Even though Kathy and her slimmer sister Barbara have 50 percent of their genes in common (as do all siblings), their risk for binge eating disorder might be quite different. Still, the evidence is fairly clear that family members of someone with binge eating disorder are over twice as likely to suffer from binge eating disorder themselves— just like having a family history of heart disease or diabetes.[1]

Over the past twenty years, researchers in genetic epidemiology, including myself, have combed through countless family profiles to show that eating disorders track through the generations. We learned that relatives of people with anorexia and bulimia are seven to twelve times at higher risk for an eating disorder—about the same rate as the risk for inheriting a tendency toward bipolar disorder and schizophrenia. Researchers have also learned that binge eating disorder runs in families.

However, family studies have a limitation: They can tell us if a trait runs in a family, but they can't tell us why. It could be because someone has inherited genes that influence a disorder, but it could also be because a child witnessed binge eating in a parent and learned those behaviors through a process called modeling—just the way you might learn how to swing a baseball bat from watching your dad play softball. So family studies can't separate genetic influences from environmental ones.

The best way to identify whether there is a genetic component is with twin and adoption studies. Identical twins are basically clones—for most intents and purposes, they share identical sets of genes. Genetically speaking, fraternal twins are no different than regular siblings. Like Kathy and Barbara, they share 50 percent of their genes, but unlike Kathy and Barbara, they grew up in the same environment (starting with their shared time in the womb). So the only thing that differs between identical and fraternal twins is the percentage of genes they have in common.

Let's consider an example. My first child was born when we lived in an apartment in Pittsburgh, Pennsylvania, in the winter. He was born into a family of two adults. My third child was born in the summer in Christchurch, New Zealand. She was born into a family of two adults and two children. Not only were they born on different continents in different seasons, they were also born into different families. Even the food that was available to me during the pregnancies differed dramatically. My children share 50 percent of their genes, but they were exposed to very different environments even before birth. Since twins develop together in the womb and are born into the same family at the same time, they share their environmental legacy.

Since the only difference between identical and fraternal twins is the percentage of genes they share, twin studies are able to isolate genetic from environmental factors by comparing how much more similar identical twins are than fraternal twins. If, for example, in a large sample of twins, you find that both members of identical twin pairs have binge eating disorder more frequently than both members of fraternal twin pairs, it's suggests that genes might be involved.

So, how do twin studies work? The basic premise is that individuals vary—in height, in our cholesterol levels, and in whether we have binge eating disorder or not. What twin studies allow us to do is to place estimates on *why* we vary—an estimate of how much is due to genes and how much is due to environment. The proportion that is due to genes is known as *heritability*.

In 1998 I was part of a group of researchers who reported that based on data about thousands of sets of twins, the heritability of the symptom of binge eating could be estimated to be somewhere between 46 and 82 percent.[2] Next, several Norwegian researchers and I wanted to move this estimate beyond looking at just the symptom of binge eating and closer to truly understanding how much genes contributed to binge eating disorder. To do this, we turned to a sample of over eight thousand sets of same-sex and opposite-sex twins in a Norwegian registry to see how much genes and environment contribute to the actual binge-eating syndrome.

Our study, published in 2004, confirmed that the syndrome of binge eating disorder also appeared to have a substantial genetic component.[3] For both women and men with the disorder, the heritability was around 47 percent. Family studies tell us that the disorder runs in families, and twin studies tell us that genetic factors influence why the disorder runs in families, but neither of those types of studies tells us which genes we are talking about, where they are, or how they work. So the field has moved forward, to developing techniques that allow us to identify the genes and what they do. With the completion of the Human Genome Project, by 2003 more than twenty-four thousand genes in human DNA have been identified.

In linkage studies, we try to narrow the search for culprit genes to particular areas on particular chromosomes. It sometimes astonishes people to hear that for eating disorders—which have been considered to be largely cultural phenomena for decades—we have identified areas on the genome where these risk genes might lie. We have made a lot of progress in linking certain traits on certain chromosomes to anorexia nervosa and bulimia nervosa, and studies on binge eating disorder are not far behind.

The Delicate Dance of Genes and Environment

Fighting the tendency to binge eat is a psychological struggle that pits your rational mind against your biology. But it's not all due to genes—your environment also plays an important role in your relationship with food. The intricate dance of genes and environment influences how at risk each of us is to succumbing to urges to binge.

Teasing out genetic factors from environmental ones is tricky business, in part because under most conditions the same people who give you your genes (your parents) also provide you with the environment in which you are raised. A classic example is IQ. Children of high IQ parents are more likely to have high IQs than children whose parents have lower IQs. Even though we know that intelligence is inherited, there is a hitch. Parents who are smart also tend to provide their children with rich and stimulating environments. They are the ones who buy Baby Mozart tapes, read to their children, and supply stimulating toys, so their kids have a "double advantage." They inherited genes for intelligence, but they were also exposed to an environment that stimulated their minds.

Unfortunately the opposite scenario can happen as well—instead of a double advantage, children can get a double disadvantage. For example, a child who inherits the risk for binge eating disorder might also grow up watching Mom and Dad restrict calories at dinner, then eat their way through a bag of cookies an hour later. Not only might the child have increased genetic risk, she or he also has been exposed to unhealthy eating habits, maybe never learning what a healthy portion size or a normal eating schedule is.

Remember Tish whose father once offered her five dollars for every pound she lost in grade school? Turns out her father was bulimic for much of her formative years. Recalling a period when she was growing up and lived with her father, Tish describes how every night after dinner he would put down his fork, invite Tish for a walk across their property, pick an orange from one of their many orange trees, and after a few slices, make himself throw up before walking back home.

At the time, of course, Tish thought nothing of it; she had no barometer to tell her whether this was normal or abnormal behavior. Today, of course, she realizes her own eating disorder is linked closely to her father's. I don't know whether the link is genetic or environmental, although I personally suspect it's a classic case of a double disadvantage.

One study we did looked at the way in which mothers with eating disorders fed their babies and toddlers. Normally moms (and dads!) go to all sorts of crazy lengths to get their children to engage in eating—making faces, playing games, singing songs, opening their mouths as the spoon gets closer to the baby's mouth. It is an emotionally engaging, interactive experience.

But that's not true of many mothers with eating disorders. When we videotaped how they fed their kids, all that came across was stress and anxiety. There was no facial expression, no engagement with their children. It was perfectly clear that eating was an uncomfortable act for them. Mealtimes were tense.

In the case of these mothers with eating disorders, the result is that adults with dysregulated eating often have difficulty knowing what healthy, normal eating is for their children. Even though as parents we're supposed to model healthy eating, if we have difficulty doing it for ourselves, we're in a tough spot when trying to teach our children. But with help, the cycle can be broken—even children who are genetically predisposed to binge eating disorder don't have to fall into the same eating traps as their parents.

Someday science may have progressed to the stage at which the genes that influence your urge to binge can be identified and maybe even functionally altered to make it easier for you to change your behavior. We're not there yet, but we know your genes are involved, which helps us better understand the battle you face. Our job is to arm you to fight the battle in the most effective way possible—to help yourself and future generations.

Binge Eating and Your Cultural Environment

What happens when there is a rapid and extreme shift in the environment? In recent years with the globalization of both the food and the entertainment industries, cultures that previously have been isolated from the bombardment of fast food and our culturally sanctioned thin ideal have become barraged by excess calories, fat, sugar, and images already widespread in the Western world. As you might expect, the results aren't pretty.

Whereas the shift was relatively gradual for us (Kentucky Fried Chicken and McDonald's arrived in the 1950s, and nowadays most suburban turnpikes are literally lined with fast-food establishments), many other countries—especially in Asia and Eastern Europe—got a rapid influx of many such establishments. (Merely eleven years after the first set of golden arches appeared on the Ginza in 1971, McDonald's became the biggest restaurant chain in Japan.)

The same was true for the cultural "thin ideal" in the international fashion industry. We first encountered the ninety-one-pound Twiggy, arguably the first supermodel, in 1966, and she was an anomaly. But then gradually the thin ideal became the norm, leading to the chic trend of the 1990s and frank emaciation by the 2000s.

Along with these changes in the environment, in the United States we saw an increase in both obesity and eating disorders. But these changes occurred over the course of just a few generations. Since our gene pool can't change that fast (it takes many many generations to see changes in the gene pool), what you are seeing is how changes in the environment can lead to different expressions of genes that have been there all along.

Let's take Fiji as an example. Dr. Anne Becker of Harvard University conducted a telling study on the island. She first studied girls' eating habits on Fiji in 1988 and then returned in 1995. By 1998 she had visited again and this time found a sharp rise in disordered eating behaviors and body dissatisfaction among those girls.[4]

What had happened in the interim? Television made its way to the island. In her 1998 survey, taken thirty-eight months after TV arrived on Nadroga, Fiji, 11.3 percent of girls, aged seventeen on average, reported that they had vomited to control weight in comparison to 0 percent who reported this behavior in 1995. Plus, 29 percent of schoolgirls scored high on an eating disorders test in comparison to 13 percent in 1995.

Showing the power of the tube, in 1998, 74 percent of the Fijian girls reported feeling "too big or fat." And if they watched TV at least three nights per week, they were 50 percent more likely to see themselves as too fat, and 30 percent more likely to diet. A full 62 percent of Fijian high school girls in 1998 reported dieting in the past month, which is astonishing in a culture that historically has valued voluptuous bodies and generous feeding. Girls with rounded Pacific Islander bodies suddenly wanted to be thin and svelte. What shows were they watching? *Melrose Place* and *Beverly Hills 90210*, among others. So the genes that influenced risk for these behaviors were there all along, but they may have been unleashed by environmental triggers such as the images of Heather Locklear and Tori Spelling.

Genes work in many ways, including making you more sensitive to the people and places in your environment. Some people can walk around in a daze, oblivious of the world around them. Nothing penetrates their protective shell and environmental insults bounce off them like water off a duck's back. Others are more like emotional Velcro. Environmental triggers stick in their craw; they carry them around and have difficulty shaking them loose. Environmental insults get under their skin like a nasty splinter.

Here's an example: Two sisters (both reasonably healthy weight) are walking down the street in the summer wearing shorts and tank tops. A car drives by filled with teenage boys. One calls out, "Look at the fat cows on the side of the road!" Sister #1, who has that protective shell, flips them the bird, utters some choice phrases herself, and goes back to her conversation with her sister. The only thing she takes from the event is "guys can be real jerks."

Sister #2, the Velcro type, outwardly agrees with her sister, but the comment gets under her skin. When they get back home, she looks at herself critically in the mirror, grabs the skin around her waist to see how much she can pinch, and wonders, "Maybe he's right, maybe I do look like a fat cow." Later, she picks up a popular magazine and goes on a crazy fad diet. By the end of the week, her body is dehydrated and screaming out to be fed. She can't take the restriction any longer and dives into a pint of Ben and Jerry's, then moves on to a bag of chips . . . and thus begins the starve-binge pattern. Meanwhile, Sister #1 continues eating normally and catalogues the whole incident with the boys and the car as completely forgettable.

The theory is that not only do genes influence your baseline

RUNNING THE RAT RACE?

As reported in *Science Daily*, University of Alabama at Birmingham (UAB) psychologists have developed an animal model for binge eating disorder.[5] The Sprague-Dawley rat model could lead to the identification of physiological mechanisms that distinguish different types of eating disorders and to the creation of new, targeted drug therapies.

In the study, published in the September 2007 issue of the *International Journal of Obesity*, UAB psychologists identified rats who are predisposed to binge on large quantities of delicious food—sugary and high-fat junk foods—in a short period of time. Of note, this pattern of binge eating, however, did not predict susceptibility to become obese, just as some human binge eaters become overweight whereas others do not.[6]

risk of becoming a binge eater, they also influence how vulnerable you are to environmental influences. Although you can't change your genes, you can learn strategies to develop more of a protective shell and keep those triggers from getting under your skin.

How to Harness Your Biology and Environment to Achieve Health

We've been talking about genetic and environmental factors that increase your risk of developing binge eating disorder, but how about ways in which your genes and the environment can buffer you from developing binge eating disorder?

Basically, this is a bit like a poker hand: You get dealt some bad cards, but you also get dealt some good cards, and then a lot of other factors come into play as well—like how good the other players' hands are, the conditions under which you are playing, and the choices you make along the way. Even though we've focused on risk genes, genes also provide us with amazingly positive features, visible things such as your beautiful eyes and your lovely hair color or texture. They also influence more abstract things like self-esteem. How they influence self-esteem is not fully known, but twin studies suggest that genetic factors do play a role in how good you feel about yourself. Self-esteem is one of those things that can buffer you from some of those environmental insults. Sister #1 was able to flip off those boys because she felt perfectly fine about herself, thank you! Maybe that was due in part to the fact that she had a little built-in protection—her self-esteem hardwiring.

Another example of genetic protection against eating disorders is what we call constitutional thinness. This is a trait found in people who are just naturally thin. They don't have urges to binge, stop eating when they are full, and sometimes even wish they could gain weight. Since they never have to go on that first weight-loss diet, their constitutional thinness may have a protective genetic effect.

There also are protective factors in the environment that decrease your risk of developing binge eating disorder. One example is growing up in a family that ate breakfast together almost every day and taught you to start the day off the right way. Or it could be something more subtle like having parents or a partner who love you just the way you are. These positive factors can protect you from developing a disorder, but they can also be powerful forces in recovery and can help you as you work to get your eating under control.

For those people who don't have genetic or environmental protections, there are ways to learn how to rip off the Velcro that makes them unable to shake off unintentionally hurtful remarks like "I love you in your skinny jeans" and which result in a three-orders-of-fries trip to the drive-through. It isn't an easy process and change doesn't happen overnight, but in upcoming chapters I will teach you successful buffering strategies to counter the impulses driven by your biology. But learning these strategies begins with the acknowledgment that you will to some extent be battling against your hardwiring.

These new buffering strategies can be invoked against a variety of environmental cues that can trigger binge-eating-prone individuals at crucial times in their lives. For example, when Kathy is in the midst of a stressful day, she needs to have a strategy in place before she reaches the mall, where one glance at the plus size apparel racks makes her feel defeated. It's a proactive process, so she needs to keep in the front of her mind that this is going to be a challenge and that at any point her body might cry out the old solution "EAT!" but in the short and the long run, this approach would cause more problems than it would solve. That being said, Kathy also must understand that just because she's more genetically vulnerable to binge eating than many women doesn't give her a free pass to say "Forget it; it's beyond my control."

If anything, she has a window into her biology. She can use her genetic risk as a warning signal; just like weather forecasting technologies that presage extreme weather, her flashing red lights can warn her of an impending high-risk time or place. She can arm herself with mental strategies knowing that she is entering a high-risk zone.

What Can We Learn from "Binge Priming"?

In laboratory experiments, researchers are able to create animal models for binge eating, at least in terms of excessive food consumption. Of course, we have not yet developed a way to ask rats or mice whether they feel out of control when they binge!

There are three major factors that can lead to binge eating in rodents: exposure to stress, periods of food deprivation, and repeated intermittent exposure to delicious food and fluids.[6,7]

These sound curiously like human stress, human dieting, and walking through the food court at the mall!

"Binge priming" is an interesting phrase that has been coined in scientific animal literature. This refers to putting animals through repeated cycles of food deprivation followed by exposure to food that they consider to be delicious. This perfect storm leads them to overeat—not only right after the food deprivation period but even after their weight is restored. So binge priming has long-term effects on their eating behavior. This sounds suspiciously like someone who goes on a strict diet, then goes off the wagon with a yummy dessert or a high-fat meal—again and again and again over months or years or even a lifetime. This repeated pattern of food deprivation followed by a delicious falling off the wagon may in fact be priming your brain for binge eating.[8]

One fascinating fact is that these lab animals that go through these cycles of deprivation and exposure to delicious foods are also more likely to misuse drugs such as alcohol and cocaine. The understanding is that this binge-priming paradigm leads to changes in the reward circuits in the brain and affects many of the neurotransmitters in the brain associated with our experience of pleasure and reward—for example, dopamine, acetylcholine, endogenous opiates, and cannabinoids.

Experts are especially worried about adolescents who undergo these repeated cycles of dieting and overeating palatable foods because their brains are still developing and are more susceptible to reward. (That, in addition to availability, is why adolescence is such a prime time for trying cigarettes, alcohol, drugs, and sex.) The concern is that binge priming during this time might set them up not only for lifetime vulnerability to binge eating but also to substance abuse.

Playing with a Stacked Deck

Let's say (simplistically) that there are four forces at work—risk genes, protective genes, risky environments, and protective environments. Now let's translate that into poker language. Some genes (spades) and some environments (clubs) increase your risk for developing binge eating. Other genes (diamonds) and environments (hearts) decrease your risk.

The first cards dealt are when the sperm meets the egg— that's when we get our spades and clubs. Then as we mature and interact with the environment, we collect our hearts and diamonds. The end result is the hand of cards that make up our risk for binge eating disorder. Like any good hand of poker, both luck (the hand you're dealt) and skill (what you choose to do with it) play a part in responding to our genetic makeup.

What if you have three spades, a club, and a diamond? The spades (genetic risk) might predispose you to being overweight and also influence your brain reward pathways. The club (environmental risk) might have been the teasing you got about your weight back in middle school.

So far it seems as though you've been dealt a bad hand. Your spades might make you super sensitive to the sights and smells of the food court, making it a high-risk binge zone. Your sister, even though she has the same parents, was dealt one spade, one club, two diamonds, and a heart. Her diamonds have made her naturally thin and her heart is a loving husband who adores her—flaws and all! She can walk right past the food court without even smelling the Mrs. Field's cookies on her way to buy a new pair of shoes.

So if you have been dealt a lot of spades, does that mean you will definitely develop binge eating disorder? Absolutely not! Genes are not destiny. You need to take the clubs, diamonds, and hearts into account, too. Not only that, but while we can't *do* anything about the genes (spades and diamonds) yet, we *can* do something about the environment (clubs and hearts).

We can't necessarily control the negative events around us, but we can actively work to build ways to better protect ourselves when they occur. Everything you learn in *Crave* is a way to stack the deck in your favor—with more hearts.

From my perspective, your binge eating disorder can be treated regardless of the cards in your hand. For some (those dealt many spades), it will be more of an uphill battle against their biology, but if they understand that, they can tailor treatment around that hand and focus on developing skills to combat some of those hardwired symptoms.

The key is to know your cards and play smart!

PART II

Crave-ology

Here are the tools you can use to treat and conquer your eating disorder.

CHAPTER 4

What's Your Profile?

Know thyself.

      —INSCRIBED IN THE TEMPLE OF APOLLO
      AT DELPHI

No binge eater need be a prisoner of his or her genes ever again; now that we know what we're up against, we can learn to make better eating decisions and control our diet on a lifelong basis.

Profiling is an important tool, and not just on crime investigation dramas. In the case of binge eating disorder, behavioral profiles help identify, isolate, and eventually manage those troubling aspects of behavior that often unconsciously sabotage recovery. To help you both identify your own unique type and understand what you'll need to do to deal with it, I have created what I call "crave-ology" profiles.

These profiles are not scientific. Rather they come from decades of working with people who suffer from binge eating disorder (before it even had a name) and seeing patterns in the triggers that set them off and how they responded to them. Most people find there are several patterns that ring true for them.

Although each binge eating disorder is unique, I have found it fascinating over the years to see commonalities across patients. If you recognize yourself in one or more of these categories, know that hundreds of thousands of men and women share similar profiles and know that you are not so isolated and alone. If nothing rings a bell, let me know because someone out there might benefit from hearing about your profile, which they may share.

Just as important, it helps to get a handle on who you are, how you respond, and where you are most vulnerable; this is all vital information that can be used to further your recovery. If you've ever felt out of control before, during, or after a binge, knowing your triggers—a critical aspect of each profile—can help you control not only your binges but the cravings that actually trigger the binges. If you wish you could count to ten before responding emotionally to food—or to the people and emotions you associate with food—knowing your vulnerabilities, thanks to your profile, can help you get a handle on not just your actions, but your emotions as well.

The Moody Blues Binger

The Moody Blues Binger is the binge eater for whom food and mood seem to be completely intertwined. Remember Luis from chapter 2? The minute his mood started to slip, he lost motivation to use any of the tools he had learned to control his binge eating. It all just seemed to require too much effort; in the face of his depressed mood, he was unable to resist the cravings and urges to binge.

Depression is most often an episodic disorder. Someone might go for weeks, months, or even years without an episode. But the darkness of depression can descend again and he or she can slip back into a negative mood state. Depression is marked by either pervasive low mood or loss of interest in things you normally enjoy (technically called anhedonia) for a period of two weeks or more. This is not just a passing bad day or even a "blue weekend"; when depression strikes, you truly can't shake the dark mood.

In addition, there are physical signs that accompany depression, such as weight gain or loss, appetite increase or decrease, insomnia or hypersomnia (too much sleep), agitation (feeling irritable and jumpy), retardation (actually feeling slowed down physically), and, occasionally, feelings of not wanting to live or desiring to end one's life. Much like binge eating disorder, depression comes in all levels of severity. Not everyone has all of the symptoms, and for some people the symptoms are more severe and frequent than for others.

Another pattern seen with depression is called dysthymia. This is a presentation in which the low mood and/or loss of interest lasts for over two years. It does not have an episodic pattern but is long-term, smoldering, and persistent. Some very unlucky people get both dysthymia and depression. Their pattern includes episodic drops below the already chronic low level of dysthymia.

But what does this have to do with binge eating disorder? Well, we know from the literature that depression is common in individuals with binge eating disorder. A recent large community study conducted in St. Louis reported that people with binge eating disorder were at substantially elevated risk for depression, generalized anxiety disorder, panic attacks, and past suicide attempts. This was not the case in obese individuals who did not have binge eating disorder. Not only that, but individuals who had binge eating disorder scored lower on a rating scale called "mental health-related quality of life." This means that their binge eating truly took a toll on their psychological well-being.[1]

We can also take a look at families to get a sense of what other problems associated with binge eating disorder cluster in family members. We find, for example, that a member of a binge eater's family is more at risk for depression than family members of people *without* binge eating disorder.[2] What this tells us is that for many people, binge eating disorder and depression go hand in hand and run together in their families. This is the hallmark of the Moody Blues Binger.

On a practical level, this means that both problems (binge eating and depression) deserve attention and that they need to be approached together. Just treating your depression might help your binge eating disorder, and just treating your binge eating disorder might help your depression, but the best solution is to address both and get both your mood and your binge eating under control.

The Angry Binger

Despite having a successful career, Estelle had never learned the skills to address conflict directly. She let people walk all over her and, take advantage of her, and instead of standing up for herself, she just "absorbed it all." One particular morning, her son had forgotten to take out the trash before he left for school (so she had to do it and got her suit dirty in the process), her husband was supposed to take the car in for repairs but forgot (Do I have to remind him about everything?), it was raining and her daughter had taken her umbrella and not returned it (Why can't people leave my things alone?) and her secretary called in late because her child was sick (Why always on the days I need her most?). It wasn't even nine A.M. and Estelle could already feel her blood pressure rising and her teeth clenching. She knew it was just going to be one of those days.

Rather than dealing with all of these minidramas directly, Estelle just suppressed her angry feelings. She had adopted the philosophy "if you want something done right, you have to do it yourself," yet she developed mounting resentment of the people around her for not helping her with the tasks that needed to be done at home and at work.

We all have an "internal voice" that is sometimes whispering in our heads, but Estelle had an incessant angry patter going on in her's: My husband is incompetent, my kids are taking advantage of me, my secretary slacks off whenever she gets a chance, and, her personal favorite, I'm the only one who does any work around here. Her resentment was eating away at her, but she was afraid to confront any of these people vital in her life directly with her feelings.

Her solution was to eat. That evening, both kids had after-school activities and her husband was working late, so she brought home a one-pound bag of M&M's and dug in. At first, the thoughts in her head were angry ones: Screw them all, I deserve at least this; it's the only pleasure I have. Gradually the anger faded away as she zoned out in her self-induced chocolate buzz. But the next morning, more things went undone; again she could not confront her family in a healthy way, and she felt disgusted by the weight she would no doubt gain from her M&M's binge.

For many people, looking conflict in the face, dealing with it directly, and expressing anger toward others are extraordinarily difficult things to do; most of us avoid confrontation if at all possible. Whether this stems from family environments in which it was not okay to express anger or from the fear that people won't like you if you get angry with them, or if you are simply afraid of being assertive and don't have the skills to do so, letting anger and resentment fester without resolution is surefire emotional poison and a common binge-eating trigger. In fact anger and hostility are two of the top emotions associated with problematic eating episodes.

The fascinating question is, how do we expect binge eating to resolve anger? As we see with Estelle, maybe there is a temporary reduction of the gnawing negative feelings, but they rush back with a vengeance when she invariably faces the same challenges the next day. The *only* problem that eating can solve is hunger.

We have, however, elevated food to a truly emotional, versus purely physical, experience. Food is our reward, our solace, our comfort, our company, our escape hatch, and our ejection seat. Once eating becomes viewed as a solution to problems other than hunger, our wires have become crossed.

For Estelle, her internal state of anger has become a cue for binge eating. When she starts having those negative thoughts about everyone letting her down, that should be a cue for assertive action—not M&M's. She is not hungry, she is angry; she must address the emotion she is feeling.

Instead of taking out the trash herself and messing up her suit, she should have said, "Len, you forgot to do your weekly chore this morning, so I need you to drive the trash to the dump this afternoon." Instead of grumbling about her forgetful husband, she should call him and say, "Honey, it was on your plate to have the car repaired; I need you to take responsibility for getting it into the shop this week. As soon as you know when it's going in, let me know so I can plan accordingly." Instead of swallowing her anger toward her secretary, she needs to have a frank performance review and provide clear expectations and feedback. These are assertive actions that will eventually get results; that one-pound bag of M&M's will never solve her problems, it will only add to them.

Being assertive isn't always easy and takes time and practice. But there are few things more rewarding than getting your hand out of the M&M's bag and choosing the assertive option in order to bring about positive change.

The Low Self-Esteem Binger

"I already suck, so I may as well make myself feel worse." This twisted logic seems incomprehensible, but to the Low Self-

Esteem Binger it makes perfect sense. The logic of a healthy person would be if you are feeling bad about yourself, do something to make yourself feel better. But that logical response is often elusive.

When we look at internal triggers for binge eating, low self-esteem is often high on the list. Low self-esteem attacks can happen to vulnerable individuals as a result of any number of insults to their self-perception—a bad grade on a test, stepping on the scale, a less than stellar performance on any task, a bad-hair day, an unpleasant social interaction, a dressing-down at work. All of these things and many more have the potential to devastate the vulnerable individual's self-esteem.

Rather than responding to these insults with an action that would be directed toward improving self-esteem, the Low Self-Esteem Binger intensifies the fall by making himself feel even worse by bingeing. As his brain hurls insults his way, food seems to be the only, albeit temporary, solace for his misery. But the key word here is *temporary*.

In this case, the intervention is clear: Target the self-esteem. Wallowing in a binge will only exacerbate the problem. Direct action is required to help the Low Self-Esteem Binger recognize and nurture healthier perceptions of who he is and what he can contribute to the world.

The Nail-Biting Binger

Stress, anxiety, and tension. These are the triggers—both chronic and acute—for the Nail-Biting Binger. Let's use Ronald as an example. Under constant financial stress, he is desperately trying to squirrel away money to send his kids to college while at the same time balancing the copays for medical bills from his parents' hospital stays. His job is not secure; he constantly sees colleagues being laid off or "downsized."

Ronald regularly wakes up in the middle of the night in a

state of panic, trembling under the burden of responsibility. He is sandwiched between two generations and feeling both responsible for—and apprehensive about—both.

Not only does the responsibility weigh heavily on his shoulders, but he also has no outlet to discuss his fears or share the burden; the anxiety builds up but has nowhere to go. Ronald developed a pattern of spending Sunday mornings poring over bills while downing doughnuts and coffee—heavy on the doughnuts. He retreats to his study with a dozen of them, prepared to do battle with his uncertain emotions the only way he knows how.

How will Ronald ever save himself? Much as Estelle needs to stand up to her family, friends, and colleagues to stop being the Angry Binger, Ronald needs to find alternative strategies to relieve stress if he wants to quit being the Nail-Biting Binger.

He can hardly blame his parents and children; chances are if either generation knew the stress Ronald was under they would sit him down and have a heart-to-heart to put his mind—and his frazzled emotions—at ease. Like Estelle—and so many other vulnerable men and women—Ronald is using food to address all the problems it isn't designed to cure. Food fixes hunger, not anxiety. In fact, for those with binge eating disorder, food is often the cause of anxiety, never the solution.

Rather than facing another Sunday with another dozen doughnuts, Ronald needs to acknowledge that he can't bear up under this constant load of pressure—his rising blood pressure attests to that fact. If his health fails, he won't be of any help to either his children or his parents. He is only human and has to realize that.

What can he do actively to alleviate the stress that is causing his binges? Perhaps, instead of socking away money for both his parents' medical bills *and* his children's college education each month, he can alternate between the two on an every-other-month basis. Or he can have a frank discussion with his siblings about getting some help from them for his parents.

These may not be the ultimate solutions, but they will immediately alleviate some of his stress and possibly enable him to relax enough to come up with more alternatives—and that might be enough to save him from that nail-biting binge.

The Running-on-Empty Binger

In the study we conducted with *Self* magazine recently, 37 percent of women between the ages of twenty-five and forty-five endorsed skipping meals as one of their most frequent approaches to weight control.[3] Well, what about that? We've already blown the trumpet for a good breakfast, but what harm could there possibly be in skipping lunch? Let's look at Lucy and see how skipping lunch turned her into a Running-on-Empty Binger.

Lucy did the right thing in the morning: She had a passable breakfast consisting of a piece of toast, four ounces of orange juice, a small low-fat yogurt, and a cup of coffee. But truth be told, even downing this "sensible breakfast" scared her. She was afraid that if she had breakfast *and* lunch, there was no way she could possibly eat dinner, too, without ballooning to huge proportions. So she developed a daily pattern of skipping lunch entirely, with the exception of a one P.M. coffee (with nondairy creamer and noncaloric sweetener) to help her make it through the day.

By the time Lucy got the mail at three thirty P.M. and distributed it to everyone, she would start to feel antsy. Sitting in traffic on the way home was a recipe for a headache and usually prompted downing an ibuprofen or two. She hated cooking, so she would head to the prepared food section of her local grocery store. By the time she usually got there it was six P.M. and she hadn't eaten anything for the past twelve hours.

The daily patter in her head was predictable and upsetting: I'm starving; I have to stand in the checkout line, and of course

I skipped lunch so I can get that slice of pie for dessert. And maybe I should buy the whole pie, because it's cheaper than buying just a slice and probably fresher, too. I better grab a loaf of bread while I'm here, and I like those spicy chips . . .

So she checks out and before she can get the food home, she has ripped open the bag of chips in the car. Predictably, Lucy says she'll "just have a few" to take the edge off of her hunger, but the bag is empty by the time she gets home. She sits down at the kitchen table with the mail, mindlessly going through it while she wolfs down her turkey tetrazzini, green bean casserole, and her first slice of pie, then her second—and her third. And before she knows it, there's only one slice left. She tries doing the mental math to see if skipping lunch really "earned" her that many calories, but not surprisingly it didn't even come close. By running on empty all day, all she did was set herself up to binge and ride roughshod over her satiety signals.

The same pattern holds in lab animals in binge-priming experiments. Much like the Running-on-Empty Binger, they eat more food after food deprivation and stress than they do when they were being fed a satisfying, regular diet.

A famous experiment conducted by Ancel Keys showed this decades ago when he studied the effects of food deprivation on men who were conscientious objectors during the Second World War.[4] This study has been incredibly valuable in understanding the effects of food deprivation on human beings. During the experiment, the participants were subjected to semistarvation diets in which most lost more than 25 percent of their weight, and many experienced anemia, fatigue, apathy, extreme weakness, irritability, neurological deficits, and lower extremity edema (swelling).

This experiment has been a veritable treasure trove of information on food deprivation, including looking at what happens to appetite after food deprivation. Although the experimenters warned the participants to be careful not to overeat after a rehabilitation period, they were free to eat as they chose. In 2003–

2004, eighteen of the original thirty-six participants were still alive and were interviewed. Some of them recalled what happened when the controls were removed.

One participant reported having to go to the hospital to have his stomach pumped because he "just simply overdid" eating. Another reported getting sick on a bus after an early meal and said he simply "couldn't satisfy [his] craving for food by filling up [his] stomach." Other participants reported prolonged periods of eating excessively after they left [the study]; and one man described the feeling as a "year-long cavity" that needed to be filled. A year-long study is more extreme than skipping a few meals, but the principle is the same. Running on empty not only impairs your functioning but also causes you to overeat once you have access to food again.

To enable your body to predict when and how much food is being ingested it's helpful to maintain as regular a schedule as possible. I remember when I was learning how to drive, my dad told me never, ever let the gas tank get below a quarter-tank full. His logic was you never know when you are going to get stuck in traffic or have an emergency or run into a snowstorm, so it's best to just ignore that big red *E* on the extreme left and, instead, pretend that "1/4" is your *true* empty line. I've followed his advice to this day and have never run out of gas.

The same logic holds for meals. It's better have an apple when your tank is getting low than to wait until you are in the red zone and on the path toward a binge.

The Bedroom Binger

What we did in various rooms of our house used to be well-defined. We ate in the kitchen or dining room, slept (and engaged in other enjoyable activities) in the bedroom, and watched TV in the den or living room. I fondly remember the following admonitions from my childhood: "No eating in the living room" and "If you're going to fall asleep, then go to bed."

Interestingly, these boundaries started to change with the advent of the TV dinner. In 1953 Swanson invented the TV dinner as a convenience for busy housewives. With the it came the "TV tray." Suddenly, America was eating dinner in the den on little tables in front of the TV set!

Sadly, this was also the beginning of the breakdown of the boundaries defining the dining room. As we got more and more TVs in our homes, we were suddenly munching on pretzels—or decidedly less healthy snacks—in the bedroom while watching TV. There was a complete breakdown of the functionality of the various rooms in the house, and *every* room became a dining room.

The Bedroom Binger is especially susceptible to this trend. To her, the bed can be set just like a table; perhaps an all-you-can-eat buffet might be the more appropriate description. With foods elaborately arranged all around her on the bed the Bedroom Binger can indulge while she watches a movie or TV show, although she sometimes just binges in silence.

I worked with one woman who would carefully plan her bedroom binges. She looked forward to these evenings on her queen-size bed with her favorite binge foods so much that it was like planning a special night out. She chose her nightclothes in advance (nothing too tight), ignored the phone all evening if it rang, and basically crafted a sheltered environment in which to enjoy her binge.

It always began quite enjoyably for her. Those first bites as she sat on her sumptuous bed gave her a sense of pleasure and calm. As the evening progressed, her feelings would transform from pleasure into guilt and often she would just fall asleep surrounded by food remains, wrappers, crumbs, and various stains and spills.

Much like an alcoholic who's had too much to drink, she would basically "pass out" during the binge, then sometimes wake up in the middle of the night, roll over in her own food mess, and feel repulsed by what she had done. She once told me that it was like waking up next to someone you didn't know, wondering how you had ended up in a stranger's bed, and being disgusted with yourself for what you had done. Like a one-night stand—with food—only for her it was more like a longtime love affair. These nights would be followed by days of self-loathing and embarrassment. She wondered what people would think if they could see a video of her pathetic behavior.

To stop the bedroom bingeing, she had to do two things: First, find something to replace that initial pleasure and calm that she was looking for when she planned the binge. This is what seduced her into this behavior and this is what she looked forward to. She did this through trying a series of options that she felt might be able to bring her the calm and relaxation she was seeking.

Somewhat to her surprise, what ended up working was planning an evening alone with candles and a good book. Only the "good" book wasn't the type of more intellectually satisfying book she normally chose. She let her guard down and allowed herself to get some lowbrow books for these special evenings. She found that she was able to enjoy just turning her mind off for a few hours and not feeling bad about it the next morning.

The second fix harked back to pre-1953 and involved establishing some boundaries in her house. She learned to distinguish the bedroom from the kitchen/dining area and stuck to the adage "I won't eat in your bedroom if you don't sleep on my kitchen table." Sometimes what works best is what's most conventional and familiar.

The Midnight Binger

The Bedroom Binger is not to be confused with the Midnight Binger, although they *can* coexist. We have been hearing more and more about the syndrome of night eating. Like binge eating disorder, night-eating syndrome (NES) is not yet an official diagnosis, but considerable work is being done to characterize the syndrome. People with NES tend to do the majority of their eating after traditional dinnertimes, so often over half of their daily food intake occurs after most of us have stopped eating for the evening. People with NES will often wake up in the middle of the night and eat. The Midnight Binger takes NES one step further and actually wakes up in the middle of the night to *binge*.

Perhaps unsurprisingly, the Midnight Binger complains frequently of sleeping problems and lack of appetite in the morning. We know that NES is associated with depression and body image distress, so the Midnight Binger probably has the same concerns.

We just don't know how common NES is because most published studies are small or have been conducted on clinical samples. Some of the questions asked to determine whether a person has NES or is a Midnight Binger are: What percentage of your daily food intake occurs after dinner? How often do you get up at night and eat? And binge? Do you have difficulty falling asleep? Do you tend not to have an appetite in the morning?

The Midnight Binger and NES sufferer can benefit from some of the social rhythm therapy approaches discussed in chapter 5. A combination of regular eating and effective sleep hygiene can help stabilize both eating and sleeping rhythms and help bring the midnight cravings under control.

The Drive-Through Binger

You might be surprised to know that the car is one of the most frequently cited places for a binge. My colleague Carol Peterson, Ph.D., at the University of Minnesota used PalmPilots to figure out when and where overweight individuals were most likely to experience problematic eating episodes. The car ended up being one of the most high-risk venues for problematic eating.

Think about it: Just about every junk food you can imagine is available either via a drive-through window or the local convenience store. But it's not just convenience that fuels the Drive-Through Binger; privacy and anonymity play dual roles in the attractiveness of drive-through bingeing. If you're alone in your car, there's no one to watch and no one to walk into the kitchen and catch you, and you can easily pack everything up and throw it away in a public trash can, leaving no visible evidence except maybe some crumbs and stains on the car seats.

For some Drive-Through Bingers, this pattern develops out of necessity. Kathy, who was introduced earlier, was basically trapped in her car shuttling children from school and from one activity to another. When she was legitimately hungry, she felt that all she had time for was to grab something from the drive-through between pickups and drop-offs. But then she began to realize was something about her increasingly frequent, very private, and even devious drive-through binges: She started to view them as her "alone" time. She would turn off her phone, find her favorite easy listening station, and just zone out while she was bingeing.

It took a couple of close calls to shake her into the realization that it was positively dangerous to binge eat while she was operating a motor vehicle! That, coupled with two occasions on which she was actually late picking up her kids because finishing off the binge in peace and erasing her trail was more important than being there on time for her children, gave Kathy the wake-up call she so desperately needed. When she arrived and found the kids in tears because they were the last ones to get picked up, she realized that her problem had gotten out of control. What would it look like if she got in an accident or got stopped by a police officer and there were piles of food wrappers and remains scattered all over the front seat?

How humiliating, she thought. How pathetic.

In fact, no one knows just how often binge eating in the car is associated with motor vehicle accidents or near misses. Fascinatingly, in contrast to the United States, where you see people doing everything from eating lunch, putting on mascara, reading the paper, and even text messaging in their cars, in many countries it is illegal even to drink a beverage in the car, and hands-free telephones are mandatory.

In England, for example, the national highway code contains the following mandate:[5]

> Safe driving and riding needs concentration. Avoid distractions when driving or riding such as:
>
> - loud music (this may mask other sounds)
> - trying to read maps
> - inserting a cassette or CD or tuning a radio
> - arguing with your passengers or other road users
> - eating and drinking
> - smoking

America has been slow to follow such legal strategies, but can additional regulations be far from being enacted? According to the Maryland Department of Transportation[6]

> In Maryland, currently there are no specific laws prohibiting distracted driving behaviors such as eating while driving, reading while driving, or cell phone use while driving, for example. However, there are laws in the Annotated Code of Maryland that require a driver to be aware, alert and not operating a motor vehicle in an unsafe manner:
>
> - A person is guilty of reckless driving if he drives with a wanton or willful disregard for the safety of people or property.

- A person is guilty of negligent driving if he drives in a careless or imprudent manner that endangers people or property.
- Drivers also have a duty to exercise due care.
- A person may not drive on the roadway wearing earplugs, a headset or earphones over or in both ears, except hearing aids.

Many people who binge refer to getting into "binge mode" or the "binge zone." Most of the time this means that their awareness of the world around them becomes blurred, their feelings become numbed, and they experience almost an altered state of consciousness as they temporarily disappear in a sea of food. Aside from the personal implications of such behavior for the individual, zoning out is dangerous to both you and others when you are behind the wheel!

Drive-Through Bingers can break their pattern by adopting a simple prohibition. No more food in the car! Period.

The Party Hearty Binger

Most of the time when we are talking about binge eating, the focus is on all of the negative emotions that trigger a binge— depression, anxiety, low self-esteem. But what about the opposite end of the mood spectrum? How about those gregarious, outgoing few for whom the party atmosphere is the trigger that finally unleashes their appetite?

Believe it or not, there are some people for whom the exuberance associated with a party atmosphere shuts off their appetite monitors. What is it about the party atmosphere that destabilizes their eating control mechanism?

Well, for starters, most parties involve delicious foods, usually scattered around everywhere, not to mention being available for hours, which makes keeping track of what you are eating extremely difficult. Imagine a party where servers are walking around with trays of hors d'oeuvres. You grab a little napkin and a toothpick and start picking away, one tidbit at a time. Each time a server walks by you are bombarded by a food cue—a tray of yet another delicious thing to try. Everyone else seems to be sampling everything. (You are probably selectively watching the people who *do* try things and not paying attention to the people who wave the servers away politely.) By the end of the night, after the dessert trays have come around, you have no idea how much you've consumed.

What's worse, there are so many stimuli it's hard to keep track of your food consumption even when you're really, really trying. Ever try to count money while someone is talking to you? It's easy at first; then you get distracted by some comment, and just like that, you have to start counting all over again. Well, let's say you've counted four Swedish meatballs—not so bad—and three pieces of cheese when someone from across the room calls your name and engages you in conversation. Uh-oh, you think as he or she finally walks away. Was that four pieces of cheese or six meatballs? Or was it one each? Oh, look, here comes another guy in a tux holding a tray full of something that looks good. Let's wipe the slate clean and start all over again.

Let's add another party factor—alcohol. Another dynamic associated with problematic eating episodes in overweight individuals is the consumption of three or more alcoholic beverages in a night. Downing three alcoholic beverages at a party isn't hard to do. At that party offering all the delectable delights gliding around the room on numerous silver platters, they are also walking around with trays of drinks. You naturally replace your empty glass with a full one, or you put a half-empty glass down somewhere, lose it, then grab another full one, or your host is coming around and constantly keeping your glass full.

If you're engaged in conversation and caught up in the party atmosphere you probably have no idea how much you have had to drink. Meanwhile, the alcohol is working to unleash your appetite. One thing we do know is that alcohol disinhibits appetite just as it disinhibits all sorts of other things. We eat more when we are drinking, and people who have learned the skills to control their binge eating have greater difficulty applying those skills when they are under the influence of alcohol.

In addition, some of the same brain systems that are activated by sweet foods are also triggered by alcohol. Your natural opioid system responds the same way to both sweets and alcohol, and some people's more so than others.

Even though the Party Hearty Binger might begin the evening in a positive mood associated with a party, it doesn't necessarily end that way. To the outside observer, the Party Hearty Binger is caught up in the festivities of the moment, engaging with others, is maybe even the life of the party. But her internal struggle is the same as the Drive-Through Binger stuffing burger wrappers in the glove compartment, or the Bedroom Binger rolling over in a sea of snack-cake wrappers and hiding her head under the pillow in shame. For the Party Hearty Binger, what started out as fun, though, often ends up as heartburn and a hangover and regret about both excesses.

Several strategies can help the Party Hearty Binger enjoy the party without experiencing the negative aftereffects. The first is never to party on an empty stomach. Many people will starve themselves all day in order to save calories for the party. This is a setup for a binge disaster. You are so hungry when you finally get to the party that your first glass of alcohol disinhibits an already ravenous appetite and you're off and running; hello, Party Hearty Binge, here we come.

Your best defense against a party binge is to have a sensible supper before you leave home. That way, when you arrive at the party, you can meet and greet without desperately devouring whatever food is available to curb your craving. You are then empowered to make wise choices, not grab anything and everything you see.

Second, although it would be best to avoid alcohol altogether if it tends to set you off, some people find it difficult not to drink alcohol at parties. In that case, alternate. For each alcoholic beverage you drink, chase it with a glass of water, club soda, or seltzer. If it makes you feel more social, put your water in a wineglass, or have it in a tumbler over ice and with a slice of lime. You'll end up drinking half as much during the night, retaining greater control over both your food and alcohol appetites, and be doing something good for yourself—drinking water.

The Buffet Binger

A buffet can be a nasty temptation for just about anyone, but it is especially so for people with binge eating disorder. And for some people it is their *only* trigger. But what a trigger it is—food as far as the eye can see, and all at the same price whether you eat a little or a lot. I have witnessed this phenomenon around the world—from roadside restaurants along interstates to cruise ships to Swedish smorgasbords—there is something about the perception of the unlimited availability of food that removes the brakes and overrides the satiety system.

The power of the buffet was observed long ago by my esteemed colleague Albert "Mickey" Stunkard. As the discoverer of binge eating, Professor Stunkard based his science in the power of observation.[7] In a 1978 study he and his colleagues spent time in four restaurants (Italian, American, Irish, and Danish) and observed them under two different conditions: their menu nights and their smorgasbord nights. They found that in the Italian, American, and Irish restaurants, which were cheaper overall, on smorgasbord nights more obese people ate at the restaurants than on menu nights. Plus, they observed that far more food was consumed under smorgasbord conditions than under menu conditions. They concluded that this was a classic example of the unleashing of environmental controls and that obese people might actually seek out situations in which more food is available. I contend the same may hold true for the Buffet Binger.

What's the best strategy for the Buffet Binger? I recommend the plateless reconnaissance mission. Of course, the best defense is to avoid the buffet altogether, but sometimes—for example, on a cruise ship—that can be nearly impossible. The real danger lies in bellying up to the buffet with a large, empty plate in your hand. The empty plate is saying "fill me" and the football field of food is saying "eat me." This is a disastrous collision; nearly impossible for anyone to ignore, let alone the Buffet Binger. Once you heap the food on your plate, your internal tape starts playing "eat everything on your plate!" Well, you should indeed *not* eat everything on your plate—especially if it is enough for a family of five!

The plateless reconnaissance mission has you take a tour of the buffet with no plate in hand. On your tour, identify the three or four things you most want to try. Then pick a medium-sized plate (not the huge oval platters they sometimes have available), and select reasonable portions of those—and only those—things. Talk to yourself the whole time you are self-serving. Identify your targets, home in, serve, and move on. Do not let yourself get distracted by new foods that you didn't earmark on your recon tour. Walk away, look away, and stay away.

Those buffet food cues will try to lure you back. You'll naturally wonder if they have brought anything new out since your recon tour, but resist going back to look. Let the waiter take the plate away and you are done.

Coin a new vocabulary; change the meaning of the words *all you can eat*. It is not a command to eat as much of everything as you can. It is an invitation to *choose* from a variety of options.

Don't let the advertisements undermine your successful attempts to navigate the buffet so that you can leave without loosening your belt and feeling miserable because of an overindulgent food experience that took its satiety cues from the environment (i.e., no limits) rather than from your own body (i.e., stop, no more, you're going to regret this).

One note of caution for the Buffet Binger: The smorgasbord condition can mimic your home—where a variety of foods are available in large quantities. Learning those reconnaissance skills is critical for navigating not only the buffet, the cruise ship, and the smorgasbord, but also your own kitchen.

CHAPTER 5

Eat Breakfast, Hungry or Not!

Breakfast is the most important meal of the day.
—GRANDMA BULIK

Many people skip breakfast because they lack an appetite in the morning. Although they may be able to jump-start their day with a jolt of coffee, tea, or soda, it seems nearly incomprehensible to them that they could eat anything substantial, let alone a healthy meal, before noon. But as research indicates, skipping breakfast can be hazardous to your recovery from binge eating disorder.

There is a real connection between skipping breakfast and raiding the refrigerator at ten P.M. Many people with binge eating disorder have a complete shift in their circadian rhythms, the natural rhythm that most species have and that varies within a twenty-four-hour (ish) period. In other words, the natural cycles of their waking day get completely turned around so that while others are sleeping naturally, they are quite wide awake and *unnaturally* scouring the refrigerator—well after midnight.

I call this "food jet lag." It's as if your stomach has suddenly flown from New York to L.A. and lost a whole eating segment of the day, only to rediscover it later at the most inopportune times. Suddenly breakfast is lunch, lunch is dinner, and dinner is the new midnight snack.

Skipped or long-delayed meals before noon set you up for a binge later in the day, opening the door to fall back on clever rationales such as "Hmm . . . I skipped breakfast. That means I can have that extra dessert." Trying to "trade off" calories later in the day upsets the delicate balance that is your body's digestive system. You must reset your circadian clock gradually to retrain your body when to eat and when not to eat. By doing just a little now to control your eating cycle—and I'm not suggesting you start having a six-course breakfast when all you've been used to is a cereal bar during your morning commute— you can save yourself years of heartache later by nipping your circadian shift in the bud.

The circadian training table starts with breakfast; this simple meal creates a healthy foundation for the rest of the day and sets you up for success rather than failure. Success comes step-by-step: Start with small, digestible amounts and gradually build up to a proper breakfast. It's time to reset the clock and spring ahead into behavior change.

Larks versus Owls:
Stabilize Your Rhythms, Stabilize Your Binge Eating?

Many researchers consider binge eating disorder to be closely related to a disorder of circadian rhythms. In fact, several lines of evidence point to the possibility that binge eating disorder and its partner, obesity, may share some fundamental problems in terms of circadian rhythms.

You may not know the name, but you definitely know the feeling. It's what makes you drowsy in the evening and refreshed in the morning, energetic at two P.M. and a little more mellow at six. It's why you feel disoriented and zombie-like if the phone rings at four A.M. and cranky and tired if you fly across the country and find yourself at odds with the different time zones you've crossed.

For humans who are diurnal (active mainly during the day-time), waking up with the sun and sleeping by the moon is normal. We also have ultradian rhythms (those that vary more frequently within a twenty-four-hour period) that influence things such as hunger. Nocturnal animals do the reverse—they sleep with the sun and are active with the moon. Crepuscular species are most active during dusk and dawn.

We know that human rhythms vary within our diurnal and ultradian norms. Some people are morning people (larks) and some people are night people (owls). When a lark marries an owl it can require some creative household problem solving! While the lark is settling in for a quiet evening at home the owl can be itching to rev up and enjoy the nightlife. Likewise, while the lark is bounding around the house the next morn-ing, the owl is still dead asleep.

But people also vary in terms of how regular their rhythms are. If you have children you might realize that, often from birth, some kids are incredibly regular in their rhythms—they wake up at the same time every morning, get tired at the same time every night, and you can set your watch by when they want to eat! Then there are other kids who seem to be oblivi-ous to the fact that we are supposed to have these rhythms, and their biology just seems to be chaotic and unpredictable. One day they're up at six and ready to go, the next day they could sleep until noon if you let them.

People with binge eating disorder and some people who are overweight might just have some basic disruptions in these cir-cadian and ultradian rhythms. One of the first things that jumps out at you, clinically speaking, when you run a group for binge eating disorder is how many people say they don't eat breakfast.

Not only do they say they don't eat it, but they will often say things like "my stomach doesn't wake up before noon" or "eating in the morning makes me nauseated." For most individuals, when their eyes wake up, it's usually all systems go; they're ready to "break" the "fast" that occurred while they slept during the night. But it is almost as if the eyes and brains of people with binge eating disorder wake up, but their appetite and stomachs are both still sleeping. The dissociation may be hard for regular breakfast eaters to understand, but the dilemma is very real for those who say breakfast is a chore.

Unfortunately, skipping breakfast seems to lead to an uncoupling of rhythms throughout the day, with the stomach lagging behind, often by several hours. Most people get hungry around breakfast time (six to eight A.M.), lunchtime (eleven A.M. to one P.M.), and dinnertime (five to seven P.M.), then go to bed a few hours later with their tummies happy and ready for the overnight fast. For binge eaters, their stomachs might only be gearing up around lunchtime and are still running full steam ahead at bedtime. This snowball effect can lead to nighttime eating, midnight snacks, and nearly unconscious fridge raids well into the early-morning hours.

Another piece in this puzzle is the association between insomnia and obesity. Studies in both adults and children have shown that poor sleep or too little sleep is actually associated with higher BMI. Now exactly *how* this works isn't clear, but by changing your circadian rhythms back to the natural diurnal pattern and eating breakfast when you wake, lunch in the middle of the day, and dinner at night, you can regulate your binge-eating patterns and decrease your likelihood of becoming overweight.

The concept is rooted in science. In 2005 Ellen Frank, Ph.D., and her colleagues published a study on a specific type of psychotherapy for people who have bipolar disorder (commonly known as manic depression).[1] This team of investigators understood that the circadian clock was completely disrupted in individuals who swung back and forth between periods of depression and mania. Interestingly, in these patients both sleep *and* appetite were affected.

Depressed individuals fall into a couple of patterns. Some find themselves sleeping less (having difficulty falling asleep, waking up in the middle of the night, and experiencing early-morning awakening) and also losing their appetite and weight. Others experience the opposite—they sleep more (sometimes even getting out of bed at all is hard) and they experience an increase in appetite.

When people are in a manic state, most often they get by on very little sleep (sometimes less than an hour per night). So understanding the centrality of circadian rhythms to this disorder, Frank and her colleagues developed social rhythm therapy. This therapy is very directive and underscores the importance of maintaining regular social rhythms.

The regularity focuses on everything from meals to bedtime and wake-up time, to more social rhythms such as how patients interact with various family members, including parents and siblings. By identifying various social triggers—family gatherings, big dinners, job challenges—that can trigger manic or depressive episodes, social rhythm therapists can better treat their patients.

I am proposing that some of the same principles apply to recovery from binge eating disorder. Every evidence-based treatment for binge eating disorder and other eating disorders focuses on the importance of having regular meals. Try to develop regular social rhythms in order to combat your binge eating and weight problems.

Betsy and the "Boomerang Effect"

Because of her job, Betsy has to be up at six A.M. every day and at work by seven. Her appetite definitely doesn't wake up with her—in fact, she's barely awake until her first jolt of coffee at the 7-Eleven on her way to work. She says coffee is "all she can handle" that early, and she has no hunger pangs at all until somewhere between noon and two P.M., when her stomach wakes up with a vengeance and declares in no uncertain terms that it's time to eat. At that point Betsy grabs something fast, as she usually has to run errands during her lunch break. She makes it through the rest of the day, but by the time she gets home around four thirty she has only one thing in mind. She takes off her bra, jewelry, and work clothes, puts on her comfortable and expandable velour sweats and her slippers (her "eating uniform"), closes the kitchen blinds, and dives into her favorite binge foods. For a few moments, the stress of the day disappears, but it all rushes back again as her "binge hour" progresses.

I call this the "boomerang effect," because even though her breakfast is delayed, her hunger inevitably catches up with her later in the day—and in a big way. It's like a boomerang; no matter how far you "throw" it, you can outrun your natural rhythm for only so long before it comes right back and bonks you on the head.

Now the kicker is, Betsy has Saturday and Sunday off, and she views it as an opportunity to "let it all hang out." Rather than trying to keep to a semiregular schedule, sometimes on Friday evening she'll stay up until two A.M. watching old movies and then sleep in until eleven or twelve on Saturday. Then she'll do the same thing on Saturday night, wake up at noon on Sunday, and be too wide awake to go to sleep when it's time for bed on Sunday night. It's only natural; her body doesn't know what to expect after a weekend of erratic sleeping patterns! Needless to say, the drive to work on Monday morning is painful and the stop at the 7-Eleven absolutely necessary.

How can this boomerang effect be remedied? I am not suggesting you adopt a military lifestyle or one of scripted routines—breakfast promptly at six, lunch at noon, dinner at seven, with no exceptions—but you should aim to be more regular, on both weekdays and weekends, so that your body can come to know what to expect and when.

Betsy's circadian pattern actually feeds into her binge-eating patterns. Even though six is pretty early to wake up, it wouldn't be nearly as difficult on Monday if she didn't have a sleep hangover from her weekend behavior. Just starting her week, she is already burned out, stressed out, and vulnerable to a binge. That also means she will probably feel less equipped to deal with the stresses of her job on Monday, which will increase the likelihood of a Monday afternoon binge, to say nothing of the rest of the week. By not eating breakfast and by having lunch on the run, she sharply increases the odds of bingeing in the late afternoon and evening. So to address a situation like Betsy's, I have two very simple recommendations:

1. **Start training your stomach to expect breakfast.** I always say that we can't create more time, but we can certainly use the time we have more effectively. Instead of stopping at the 7-Eleven for coffee, Betsy should prepare her breakfast and preset her coffeemaker the night before. This could be as simple as putting some cereal in a bowl with a banana beside it next to the fridge. While her coffee finishes brewing she can pour in the milk and have a light, healthy breakfast before her first cup is ready. Make that cup to go, and it will actually end up taking her less time to eat breakfast than stopping at the 7-Eleven, getting her coffee, waiting in line to pay for it, and getting back into traffic.

2. **Be a little less extreme in weekend behavior.** Betsy can allow herself an extra hour in the evening to watch a movie, but she should start a little earlier and aim to get to bed around the same time she does on weekdays. For instance, most movie channels run on a two-hour cycle: one movie starts at six, the next at

---

THE FAST-FOOD INDUSTRY UPSETS OUR CIRCADIAN RHYTHMS

Breakfast all day? The fourth meal? Twenty-four-hour drive-through? Breakfast pizza? Breakfast burritos? Sausage, egg, and cheese with two pancakes for a bun? If you allow your stomach to be ruled by the various menus at your favorite fast-food restaurant(s), you might never know what time of day it is. Unfortunately, neither will your stomach.

To avoid living on fast-food time, take two weeks to reorient yourself with the natural world and restrict breakfast foods to breakfast times, lunch foods to lunchtimes, and dinner foods to dinnertimes. Not only will this help to reorient you to your natural diurnal cycle, but it should help you avoid fast food or eat less of it. It may be an adjustment, but did you really want that "breakfast pizza" anyway?

---

eight, another at ten, and so on. Often, the movies that run in the afternoon are repeated late in the evening, so if Betsy were to start watching movies earlier on the weekend, say at six or eight, she most likely wouldn't miss anything—particularly sleep! She could stay up until eleven watching a movie, get up Saturday at seven thirty or eight and have breakfast, then do the same thing on Sunday evening. This way, Monday morning won't come as such a shock to her system—and her week will always get off to a healthy start.

Skipping Breakfast Packs on the Pounds

Forgoing breakfast not only wreaks havoc with your circadian rhythms and sets you up for evening bingeing, it also contributes to weight gain, even among people who do not binge. According to a study published in *Obesity Research*, eating breakfast is a common characteristic among those who lose weight and keep it off.[2] The study reported, "U.S. researchers at the University of Colorado, the University of Pittsburgh, and Brown University routinely collected data on a group of people comprising the National Weight Control Registry (NWCR). In order to be eligible for inclusion in the registry, an individual has to have lost a minimum of 30 pounds (13.6 kg) and maintained the weight loss a minimum of one year."

The NWCR includes a variety of information on nearly five thousand individuals who, on average, "have lost 66 pounds (30 kg) and kept the weight off for over 5.5 years." Strategies that the NWCR has declared as contributing to their success include "eating a low-calorie, low-fat diet, monitoring food intake and body weight, and maintaining high levels of physical activity.

"As part of routine follow-up, the people in the NWCR were asked, 'How many days of the week do you eat breakfast?' Nearly 80% reported eating breakfast 7 days per week and only 4% reported never eating breakfast. Almost 90% said that they ate breakfast on most days of the week (4 or more days). Of absolutely critical importance, there was no significant difference between breakfast eaters and non-breakfast eaters in the number of calories they consumed during the day. That means that the old excuse that breakfast just adds extra calories holds no water. If anything, breakfast helps you regulate your caloric intake throughout the day."

In an article entitled "Energy Intake at Breakfast and Weight Change: Prospective Study of 6,764 Middle-aged Men and Women" for the *American Journal of Epidemiology*, a team of researchers documented a direct link between eating breakfast and controlling one's weight.[3] The study's participants kept a food diary for seven days and carefully recorded their "energy intake" throughout the day. According to the study, all participants gained weight over the follow-up period, but those

who consumed a greater proportion of their daily calories at breakfast gained relatively less weight.

What the researchers discovered was that the people who ate between 22 to 50 percent of their energy at breakfast had the lowest BMIs compared to those who ate only 0 to 10 percent of their energy at breakfast. They concluded that shifting eating patterns to eat more at breakfast and less later in the day could help prevent weight gain in middle-aged adults.

Breakfast also helps weight control in children. In another study entitled "Skipping Breakfast, Alcohol Consumption and Physical Inactivity as Risk Factors for Overweight and Obesity in Adolescents," published in the *European Journal of Clinical Nutrition* on November 28, 2007, researchers studied a group of 25,176 Dutch teenagers between the ages of thirteen and sixteen to determine which risk factor—skipping breakfast, alcohol consumption, or physical inactivity—was the most significant. Given all three factors, the study reported that, "Breakfast skipping showed the strongest relation with overweight . . . The most important risk factor for overweight and obesity was skipping breakfast."[4]

Skipping breakfast may lower your metabolism (making it easier to gain and harder to lose weight) and impairs concentration throughout the morning hours. That's why teachers implore their students to eat breakfast, particularly on the morning of a big test, when so much is riding on their mental alertness.

Give Your Stomach a Wake-up Call

When, how much, and how soon should you eat breakfast? I recommend that you eat breakfast within about an hour of getting up, and always make sure it contains at least some protein and carbohydrate to stabilize your blood sugar and help prolong the feeling of fullness. We will get to amounts later in this chapter, but for now know that any breakfast is better than no breakfast. It's better to eat a banana on the run than skip breakfast altogether.

If you are really in a pinch (and this happens to everyone occasionally), you can grab an on-the-go option such as a bagel, a banana, or a container of yogurt. But remember, when you are moving and eating at the same time, your stomach and your mind are not registering all of those important signals that indicate hunger and fullness. So save the on-the-go breakfasts for rare occasions only.

If you are one of those people whose stomach likes to sleep in the morning, then you need to gradually train your stomach to wake up earlier. How? One small step at a time.

The first and most important step is to allow a little extra time for breakfast, even if it means getting up ten minutes earlier. You'd be amazed by how waking up earlier allows your stomach the time to get hungry without having to rush. Start with something small and palatable that you can fix easily—a banana, a piece of toast, an English muffin, or a low-fat yogurt. We'll call that your Level 1 Breakfast.

Start with your Level 1 breakfast, but don't expect to accelerate to Level 2 too fast. You might need to stick with a Level 1 menu for a week, maybe a month, but not forever.

The goal is to get your stomach—and your brain—to become accustomed to eating breakfast and even to look forward to it. This is basically establishing a new habit by shaping it gradually. Over time, the habit will become ingrained and it won't require so much conscious effort. Remember, your ultimate goal is to have a healthy, balanced breakfast, but there's no rush.

When you're ready to start Level 1, do some self-monitoring of your urges to binge throughout the day. You want to establish a baseline pattern of those urges—especially throughout the evening. Your goal is to see how breakfast influences your urges to binge over the next twenty-four-hour period. One common side effect of eating breakfast is a decrease in your evening urges to binge.

For instance, here's how two women faced their days battling
the question of whether to eat breakfast or not, one eating it,
one going without. After learning the benefits of eating breakfast, Sylvia decided to self-monitor and begin eating breakfast,
paying special attention to whether this one critical step helped
her avoid her nighttime binges. Each morning she ate breakfast,
she wrote down her feelings about how it might help her avoid
an afternoon or evening binge. When she did binge, she wrote
down her feelings then as well.

Over the course of two weeks, she managed to wake up fifteen minutes earlier every morning and force herself to eat a
Level 1 breakfast. The size and content of her breakfasts var-
ied, but not her determination to eat them. During the first
week she felt like bingeing at night only twice; by the second
week, she binged only once and confessed in her daily journal
that it was more out of habit than anything else. After increasing her breakfasts to Level 2, she rarely felt the urge to binge
anymore.

Carol, on the other hand, found it more challenging to eat
breakfast. She had never eaten breakfast and couldn't see the
value in doing so now. She did try setting her alarm once or
twice, but the allure of ten more minutes of sleep always won out
over breakfast. Several times throughout the first week she'd
grab something on the go, but rarely finished it, and most of her
choices were of the sweet-and-sticky variety—a doughnut, Danish, or toaster pastry—rather than a slow and steady energy re-
lease type of food. As a result, her self-monitoring revealed that
her binge eating behavior was hardly affected by her breakfast
experiment.

During the second week she tried a little harder, but fell
back into the same routine of hitting the snooze button rather
than the breakfast nook. Through self-reportage, we learned
that Carol saw no significant change in the amount and size of
her late-night binges. No one, least of all Carol, was surprised.

One thing I would caution both Sylvia and Carol, and anyone

else who doesn't enjoy breakfast, to remember is that it should be a gradual process. Once your stomach starts waking up a little bit more in the morning, you can add another component. If you started with a piece of toast, add a piece of fruit. If you started with a piece of fruit, add yogurt. Then stay at Level 2 until your stomach and mind are completely comfortable. Remember, it took a long time for your eating habits to become disordered; "re-ordering" them won't happen overnight.

Reward Yourself—Just Not with Food

You will have a much better chance of maintaining your behavior changes if you take things gradually and reward yourself at each step. Although developing healthier eating patterns should be rewarding in and of itself, many of us are motivated by external rewards, too. But please, NO FOOD REWARDS!

So let's say that you manage to achieve Level 1 for a week. Before you even begin that week, plan your reward—a trip to the botanical gardens, a visit to your favorite museum, a walk with a friend—something that before you do it, during the time you're doing it, and after doing it, you say to yourself, I am giving myself this reward for having maintained Level 1 for a whole week. Good job!

It is not clear why we are so poor at rewarding ourselves. In fact, many of my patients will say that they plan a reward, they achieve their goal, and then they don't follow through on the reward! Sometimes they even minimize the accomplishment: "So what if I ate breakfast for a whole week? Whatever, no big deal, that's not worth a reward."

Well, indeed it is. Imagine if you promised your child a reward for getting all A's on her report card. She proudly brings home the report card and then you say, "Well, that's not that big a deal. If you get all A's in college, *then* you'll deserve a reward." That is a great way to de-motivate your child.

You are no different. You need to respect your accomplishments no matter how small they seem to you at the time. Otherwise, your brain won't trust you as a motivator of your own behavior, and when it comes time to move to Level 2 it will say, "There's nothing in it for me anyhow!"

Once you are settled into Level 2 and have rewarded yourself appropriately, then you can move on to becoming a regular healthy breakfast eater.

Avoid the "Food Hangover" by Eating Regularly

One of the key concepts associated with cognitive behavioral therapy for binge eating disorder and other eating disorders is normalization of eating. In some therapies, scheduled eating is prescribed: three meals a day and a specific number of snacks, tailored to your needs. These therapies also help you understand what the triggers are that contribute to erratic eating patterns.

For example, people who binge in the evening or nighttime hours often say they feel like they have a "food hangover" the next morning. Sometimes they feel like they are actually still full. In those cases, nighttime bingeing triggers skipping breakfast, and skipping breakfast is a trigger for nighttime binge eating. So this is clearly a situation in which the only way to interrupt this unhealthy pattern is to break the cycle.

How can this be done? One way is to capitalize on an evening in which binge eating does not occur. Jump on the opportunity to eat a healthy breakfast on a day when you don't have a food hangover. Then you can monitor your thoughts during the day and use that breakfast as a way to defend against any evening urges to binge that might arise. They might still surface because evening binge eating has become a habit, but if you keep up the *new* habit, the urge to binge in the evening will begin to decrease as breakfast becomes a regular event.

CHAPTER 6

Stealth Sugars and How to Reset Your "Sweetstat"

The addict is twelve years old and his drug is a soft drink, purchased from a vending machine in his school. This addict and thousands like him will attend special classes, sponsored by his school, to warn him about the dangers of drugs, tobacco and alcohol. But no one will tell him about America's other drinking problem.

—JUDITH VALENTINE, PH.D., CNA, CNC

One of the biggest challenges facing binge eaters today is the perception purported by many large food manufacturers that their products are health food or, at the very least, good for you. Many people think what they're eating—and, for the purposes of this chapter, drinking—is actually good for them, when in fact nothing could be further from the truth.

Recently *Men's Health* magazine posted its top twenty food offenders for 2007. Compiled annually, this list features "the 20 worst foods on American menus." While you might think that the biggest menu items from fast-food franchises would top the list, you'd be surprised; few of them even made the list, let alone topped it.

One of the things I found most fascinating about the 2007 list is the calorie and fat content of these foods. According to the survey, "Bob Evans Caramel Banana Pecan Cream Stacked and Stuffed Hotcakes" contain over 1,500 calories—for breakfast— and over 75 grams of fat. As *Men's Health* reports, "That's the same as . . . five Egg McMuffins."[1]

Now, few of us would consider eating five breakfast sandwiches in one sitting, yet the perception that an order of caramel banana pecan pancakes is a single meal makes unsuspecting diners see this as a valid—if somewhat indulgent— choice. They are unaware that this breakfast amounts to a full complement of daily calories for some people.

Sadly, this instance of perception defying reality seems to be as prevalent for "worst food" offenders as it does for so-called healthier choices. Popular magazines are full of "did you know" spreads where healthy foods compete with presumably unhealthy ones, only to lose out. For instance, a Wendy's Chicken Caesar Salad, with croutons and dressing, has 490 calories and 34 grams of fat,[2] while a regular-size Burger King hamburger has 290 calories and 12 grams of fat.[3] But somehow the raw facts don't sink in; most of us just plain feel better ordering the salad—even if it is jam-packed with calories and fat and our brains know that's not really the best choice.

These types of thoughts and behaviors are at the heart of many of our ingrained misconceptions about how healthful foods are, how much of them we should eat, and how often. Marketers are fully aware of our biases, our misconceptions, and our fears, and they prey on them to sell their products.

And it's not all about how well informed you are, either. There are plenty of health-conscious consumers who are completely confused about what is healthful from one day to the next. In part the nutrition field has played into that—one day eggs are the devil and the next day they have been vindicated, restored to angel status; marketing departments quickly reassess their next-year strategies and tout eggs as the new "wonder food" based on "breaking scientific research" that has "just been released." What are we to believe? Sometimes I think that much of the nutritional information we provide people can make their heads spin—especially when there are contradictory claims from different reliable and respected research institutions.

The truth about our favorite foods can be hard to swallow, but what is often worse is what you *haven't* been told about them. One of the more menacing evils we are encountering in the battle against obesity today is the insidious sweetening of our food supply. High fructose corn syrup, for example, seems to be added to just about everything these days, from "100% natural" fruit juices for our kids to so-called healthy choice smoothies and salad dressings.

"Stealth sugars" refer to sugar and caloric sweeteners that are added to all sorts of foods that you might not even suspect. In the past it was relatively safe to assume that sweet foods would have sugars in them and savory foods would not. Now that barrier is not so clear. Many of the foods that we think belong in the nonsweet category actually have sugar in them in the forms of fructose, sucrose, lactose, and maltose. These "secret" sugars can show up in the most unlikely products, products once considered sugar-free by millions of Americans.

You know that most fruit juices are naturally sweet, but did you know that many, including such perennial favorites as orange juice and apple juice, can contain up to five teaspoons of combined natural and added sugar per serving? And grape juice is even sweeter, clocking in at nearly eight teaspoons per eight-ounce serving. But maybe a fruit salad would contain less sugar. Wrong. Canned fruit salad can have four teaspoons of sugar per serving—and being preserved in "light" syrup only brings it down to two teaspoons per serving.

A bran muffin, often a "healthy" choice on many breakfast

menus, can have upwards of two teaspoons of sugar. Chocolate milk, often listed as one of the healthier alternatives for kids on many school and drive-through menus, can contain up to three teaspoons of sugar. And one can of soda contains nearly ten teaspoons of sugar. The list goes on and on.

During the past thirty-seven years, the number of calories adults get through beverages has nearly doubled. My colleague at UNC, nutrition epidemiologist Barry Popkin, Ph.D., in his article "The World Is Fat" for the September 2007 issue of *Scientific American*, wrote: "Over the past 20 years a dramatic transition has altered the diet and health of hundreds of millions of people across the Third World. For most developing nations, obesity has emerged as a more serious health threat than hunger. In countries such as Mexico, Egypt, and South Africa, more than half the adults are either overweight (possessing a body mass index, or BMI, of 25 or higher) or obese (possessing a BMI of 30 or higher)."[4]

Popkin cites many reasons for this increase, including the advent of electricity and more supermarkets in traditionally agricultural societies such as those in Latin America and Asia, but the influx of sugar-sweetened beverages to cultures that previously relied on water for the bulk of their drinking needs is the most predominant. Explains Popkin, "One of the biggest contributors to the obesity epidemic in the Third World is the recent popularity of sweetened beverages."

What we drink is also a pitfall for people trying to recover from binge eating. Says Popkin, "This has considerable implications for numerous health outcomes, including obesity and diabetes, as this is just adding several hundred calories daily to our overall caloric intake."

So in addition to the food we eat, we must now shift our focus to what we drink. Want to know what the "worst" drink was on that *Men's Health* top twenty bad foods list? A Jamba Juice Chocolate Moo'd Power Smoothie, which weighed in at 900 calories, 10 grams of fat, and a whopping 166 grams of sugar (that's about 34 teaspoons)! As *Men's Health* pointed out, "Jamba Juice calls it a smoothie (which evokes images in our mind of a healthy fruit-filled blender drink), but it's got more sugar than two pints of Ben & Jerry's butter pecan."

And therein lies our dilemma: Call something a milkshake, and when we're counting calories we'll avoid it like the plague; call something a smoothie and we'll flock to it, ignoring the stealth sugars and hidden ingredients that often include chocolate, peanut butter, and even ice cream.

Now, there is nothing inherently "bad" about these foods, either individually or collectively. Occasionally, a small portion of this Jamba Juice delight would be just fine, to say nothing of fruit juice or a glass of chocolate milk. The problem is that the marketing twist lures many of us busy Americans into believing that this is a "healthy option" for lunch. So the thinking might be, All I had was a smoothie for lunch and smoothies are good for me. Those thoughts might even help set you up for a binge later in the day. The thinking then might be, Well, all I had was a "drink" for lunch, so I can afford a food snack tonight. And you are off and running.

As a result of his breakthrough research for *Scientific American*, Barry Popkin was recently interviewed for *Science Talk*, hosted by Steve Mirsky. He had this to say about the pervasiveness—and danger—of our American drinking habits:

> If you think back [over the prehistory of our species], all that we consumed as a race of hominids, and later *Homo sapiens*, is water, after maybe consuming for a year or two or three breast milk in infancy . . . Those who consume water would consume less food, so we essentially evolved a system of metabolism where the beverages we consume don't affect the food we consume. Then all of a sudden you get wine, beer and other alcoholic beverages, which we had since around 10,000 B.C., and then in the last 150 to 200 years, all

the new beverages—the carbonated beverages, the pasteurized milk and so forth, and the fruit juices that are shipped in box[es], then quick crated, and we see a new generation. But even up to 1950 we consumed very few calories from beverages, and in the last 60 years, we've gone from consuming almost no calories from beverages to a fifth of our caloric intake in the U.S., and about the same in Mexico and about the same in a dozen other countries—in some less and some more—but the point is, all of those calories we consume, but it doesn't affect the food that we take in. So if you consume water, you don't gain weight; if you consume Coke or Pepsi, you gain weight, it's that simple.[5]

In fact, most diet and nutrition books completely miss the liquid boat. When those who treat binge eating disorder focus only on what people eat, they're missing a huge part of what goes into our mouths and influences our control over eating—namely what we drink.

A Bigger Problem Than We Thought

When it comes to how and what we drink, Americans are consuming less of what we need more of—beverages such as water and reduced-fat milk—and more of what we need less of—soda and sugar-sweetened drinks.

Colleagues of mine at the University of North Carolina at Chapel Hill analyzed national beverage consumption patterns for more than 73,000 Americans, age two and older.[6] According to the study, between 1977 and 2001:

• Overall, calories from sweetened beverages were up 135 percent.

- Overall, Americans got 38 percent fewer daily calories from milk.
- Americans now get an average of 144 calories a day from sugar-sweetened soft drinks and only 99 calories from milk.
- For young people aged two to eighteen, milk fell from 13.2 percent of total calories to 8.3 percent, and soda consumption doubled.
- Older Americans also drank more sodas. Those aged forty to fifty-nine increased soft drink intake from 2 percent to 5 percent. Among people sixty or older, consumption rose from nearly 1 percent to 3 percent.

"The obesity epidemic may be aggravated by the increase in sweetened beverage intake," explain the study's coauthors, Barry Popkin and Samara Joy Nielsen. "Little research has focused on the beneficial impacts of reduced soft drink and fruit drink intake. This would seem to be one of the simpler ways to reduce obesity in the United States . . . Most soft drinks were made with sucrose (table sugar) in the 1970s, while in the 1990s and currently they are made with high-fructose corn syrup."[7]

Although the obesity epidemic could be significantly reduced if Americans simply limited their intake of sweetened soft drinks and fruit drinks, our lifestyles are taking us in a direction away from our body's needs, rather than in the right direction. Think of how we live today and the numbers above become less surprising.

We grab a drink here, grab a drink there, some cold, some hot—most convenient and store-bought. At work, we drink what's in the vending machines down the hall or what's available in the cafeteria. At a quiet dinner out, the choices are about the same. Even our children aren't safe: schools are increasingly offering sweeter and sweeter drinks, even soft drinks, as acceptable choices. Many have vending machines that bring in revenue used to pay for team sports and other activities.

At college a generation weaned on junk, fast, and convenience foods during twelve years of public school suddenly finds even more fertile ground in cafeterias full of fatty, carbohydrate-rich comfort foods or late-night pizza and other fast-food deliveries straight to their dorm rooms. Aside from their more obvious alcoholic drink choices, they often grab what's comforting—and familiar—on the run: soda from vending machines or overpriced and oversweetened coffee drinks. For those who need caffeine but eschew coffee and tea, sodas have stepped in as a legitimate breakfast beverage. Even senior citizens in assisted living facilities or nursing homes are offered sodas as often as they are offered coffee and tea.

So it should come as no surprise that the daily caloric intake of Americans has increased about 240 calories per day, and two-thirds of that comes from sugar-sweetened beverages (SSBs). What *should* be surprising, however, is that drinking SSBs is associated with a greater increase in overall calorie consumption per day than can be accounted for by soft drinks alone. This suggests that something about SSBs may increase hunger, decrease fullness, or set people up to expect and consume sweeter foods. The sweeter the food, the higher the carbs, fat, and sugar content there usually is in the food itself.

This is yet another stealth hurdle that people with binge eating disorder are running into every day. They are struggling to keep their eating under control, yet the amount of sugars they are being exposed to from a variety of SSBs, including sodas, coffee drinks, fruit juices, sports drinks, and even flavored waters, is increasing on a regular basis. This reminds me of the story about the frog and the boiling water. If you toss a frog into a pot of boiling water, it will jump right out. But if you put that frog into a pot of room temperature water and then turn up the heat until the water reaches a boil, the frog will slowly adapt and eventually boil to death! So people who are vulnerable are actually getting used to these higher levels of sweeteners and perhaps even starting to crave more and more stealth sugars in order to satisfy their (growing) desire for sweets. This can completely sabotage their recoveries by making them hungrier for exactly the kind of sweet, fast, and convenient foods (i.e. starchy, fatty, processed) that can often derail an otherwise sensible eating plan.

It's one thing to reach for something you know isn't so good for you and expect the resulting consequences; it's quite another to reach for something you think is healthy and get those same unfavorable results. One real danger of getting burned by these so-called healthy flavored waters or natural fruit drinks is that people can develop a defeatist attitude, feeling that even their good food choices turn out to be bad. And as we all know, recovering from binge eating disorder is hard enough without *another* reason to feel disappointed, disillusioned, or even derailed.

A National Epidemic of Sweetness

Our attraction to sweetened drinks starts young. According to the National Soft Drink Association (NSDA), "consumption of soft drinks is now over 600 12-ounce servings (12 oz.) per person per year. Since 1978, soda consumption in the US has tripled for boys and doubled for girls. Young males age 12–29 are the biggest consumers at over 160 gallons per year—that's almost 2 quarts per day. At these levels, the calories from soft drinks contribute as much as 10 percent of the total daily caloric intake for a growing boy."[8]

The societal trends that drive Americans to consume more, almost unconsciously, are wreaking havoc on future generations. It is up to us to stem the tide. We have to take a close, hard look at the manufacturers of some of this country's most dangerous and prevalent SSBs. We must hold them to the highest standards of responsible marketing.

During a recent Global Obesity Business Forum at the

University of North Carolina at Chapel Hill, we were fortunate enough to have representatives from many of the nation's leading food, fast-food, and soda companies in attendance. These corporate powerhouses were joined by many researchers in the nutrition and obesity fields. Having all of them in the same room at the same time was an exciting and enlightening opportunity.

I give the companies credit for acknowledging the problem and addressing the responsibility they have in their various roles while literally feeding our country. Yet the vast differences between the industry and academic groups were best illustrated by a question that was posed by an industry participant. He asked us, quite seriously: "What would you rather have us give an obese child? Regular soda or diet soda?"

The academics looked at each other and responded immediately and unanimously "neither" and suggested water or skim milk as an alternative. This alternative, call it "Option C," wasn't really on the radar screen of these industry leaders, but was the clear and only choice from the nutritionists' perspective. But our universal answer highlighted the difference between how corporate America thinks about product placement and how easy it is for people with eating disorders to fall prey to their limited perspective. For the soda manufacturers, there are only two choices: regular or diet. From my standpoint, there are always many more choices, but it is up to the consumer to make them.

The various subtle ways in which marketing tortures those suffering from eating disorders—and consumers in general—make recovery from an eating disorder all the more challenging. Another of the latest marketing spins takes one of our most well-known nutritional recommendations and turns it on its head. You have all heard the advice to drink eight glasses of water a day. Well, that *is* good advice, but the marketing geniuses on Madison Avenue have managed to change the definition of "water."

Walk down the water aisle of your supermarket (decades ago the only water people bought at the supermarket was distilled for their steam irons!) and you will encounter a dizzying array of water and waterlike liquids. Which is the real thing? If the marketing whizzes have their way, we'll never know; they convince us that the various flavored and sweetened waters "count" toward our eight glasses per day, but what else are we getting in those products along with our H_2O? The "pseudo" waters often contain artificial flavors and artificial sweeteners—not to mention a variety of preservatives—that over time may work to desensitize our taste buds to the point where real unflavored natural water no longer tastes appealing.

With so many options available, people have the option to say, "I don't like water," Think about that statement. Back in the day when all we had to drink was water, liking or disliking it simply wasn't an option. Drink water or die of dehydration; those were your two choices. The overabundance of beverage choices we are faced with today has given us the option to even consider *not* liking water. The beverage industry knows this and markets these products as water because they know we consider it healthy to increase our water consumption. They know that you'll buy your sweet water at the grocery store or vending machine instead of drinking a glass of free freshwater from the tap.

The reality, in this case, is that water is simply the vehicle by which the beverage manufacturers deliver the sweeteners and flavorings your body will come to want. After drinking so much jazzed-up water, no wonder we've begun to think that plain water tastes boring. Your body habituates to these added flavors and craves more. In short, this inhibits you from making the right choice to drink pure and free water.

You may have thought diet soda and other beverages and foods containing artificial sweeteners could be consumed limitlessly. After all, increased consumption of these "replacement" foods and drinks is often recommended as part of the effort to improve health, particularly for those concerned about weight and diabetes. But there is a downside to this "have your cake and eat it too" approach. Historically, we have had saccharin (which has a metallic taste and causes bladder cancer in mice), aspartame (beware phenylketonurics), and now Splenda, which avoids some of the more obvious health risks of its predecessors, but is 600 times sweeter than sugar.

Before these substitutes became available, a person who was overweight or had diabetes would have to avoid sweetened foods. Now we have so many alternatives that someone who's overweight or diabetic can almost pretend that he or she doesn't have these conditions. This may or may not be a good thing. We may actually have been more careful and respectful of our body's needs back when there weren't so many alternatives.

Artificial sweeteners may be useful for people with diabetes who must limit or avoid sweets as a matter of survival, but for other people with weight regulation problems or binge eating disorder, these noncalorically sweetened foods are actually making it harder rather than easier for them to control their weight and eating.

What if all of these supersweet noncaloric sweeteners actually fundamentally changed your preference for sweets such that you need more and more sweetness in order to satisfy your craving for sweet foods? Let's say you've been eating supersweet artificially sweetened yogurt and you get used to that supersweet taste. When you are offered a normally sweetened yogurt, it won't taste as good because it doesn't provide the same "sweet kick" that you've become accustomed to. So what do you do? You just might eat more of the normally sweet product in order to get your brain pleasure centers firing. That means more calories and maybe even a jump start to a binge. Addressing this issue becomes critical with the increasing sweetening of our food supply and the ongoing struggle to stem the epidemic of obesity.

The basic biology of sweet-taste preference is fascinating. From birth on, babies differ in how much they like sweets and how much sweetness they like. One theory holds that there are two types of people. They are commonly referred to as "sweet likers" and "sweet dislikers," although these are not the most scientific of terms.

Sweet likers like sweet taste and they keep liking sweets even as things get sweeter and sweeter—nothing is too sweet for them. Sweet dislikers have a ceiling. They like sweetness up to a certain concentration, but then it all becomes too much and they start saying, "Yuck, that's too sweet."

This poses a distinct dilemma in marketing departments up and down Madison Avenue. If you want to market to the whole world (which includes both sweet likers and dislikers), you don't want to go above that point where the sweet dislikers turn off—because then you would lose that share of the market—so you have to aim for the magic balance that makes everyone happy. Or you have to change where that balance is by subtly increasing the "sweetification" of the food supply.

The food industry intuitively or perhaps systematically understands the power of sweetness. Thousands of foods in our supermarkets are sweetened. Does this create a "sweetness expectation" or even a dependency that drives our desire for increasingly sweetened foods? Do we habituate to the level of sweetness and ultimately require greater and greater levels of sweetness to satisfy our sweet cravings? Are there important subpopulations who might become more vulnerable to the lure of sweetness than others? For example, might women or individuals with eating disorders be more vulnerable to the seduction of sweet taste?

We don't have the answers to all these questions regarding the impact of an increasingly sweetened food supply on our behavior and our drive to consume sweets. Strikingly little science has been conducted to determine how eating sweetened products affects our food choices and overall dietary patterns. But

BEWARE: HEALTHY CHOICES MAY NOT BE AS HEALTHY AS THEY SEEM!

From fruit juices to canned vegetable soup, breakfast muffins to seven-grain bread, it's easier to think your food choices are healthier than they really are, experts Bonnie Taub-Dix, M.A., R.D., C.D.N., and Samantha Heller, M.S., R.D., tell WebMD.

"If a label says 'Seven-Grain Bread,' it sounds pretty healthy, right? But unless that label also says 'whole grains' it's not necessarily going to be the healthiest bread choice you could make," says one expert.

Experts also say that many people think that eating a can of vegetable soup is as nutritious as downing a plateful of veggies, not realizing how few vegetables are in the soup, and how much of the nutrients are lost in processing.

Another common mistake is substituting fruit juices for whole fruits. "Are fruit juices healthier than soda? Yes. But they are also concentrated sources of sugar that don't give you anywhere near the same level of nutrients you get from whole fruits," says Taub-Dix. What's more, says Taub-Dix, if you're trying to lose weight, you won't get the same sense of fullness from a glass of juice that you will from a piece of fruit. "Instead, you'll just take in a whole lot of calories—and still feel hungry."

The solution: Whenever possible, eat whole, fresh, and unprocessed foods. Even when you eat them in smaller amounts, you're likely to get a well-rounded group of nutrients. When buying packaged foods, put at least as much time into reading labels and selecting products as you do when choosing a shower gel or shampoo.

"Don't just assume a product is healthy—even if it's in the health food section of the supermarket," says Heller. "You've got to read the labels."[9]

there is evidence to support that constantly exposing rats to sweet-tasting foods may lead to the development of symptoms similar to those seen in individuals with opiate dependence.

For example, rats put on a diet of long-term intermittent access to a sucrose solution and regular lab chow tend to increase their sugar intake and show behavioral and brain changes similar to, albeit less dramatic than, rats dependent on drugs; when food-deprived for twenty-four hours, they also show signs of withdrawal (e.g., teeth chattering, forepaw tremor, and head shakes).

There is also emerging evidence that chronic exposure to sweet foods may cause long-term changes in preference for and consumption of sweet foods, at least in children. For example, in some countries infants are fed sugar solutions to calm them. There is some evidence that this early practice leads to stronger sweet-taste preference later in life, compared with children who have not been fed with sweet water as infants. Such early exposure may influence our sweet-taste preference throughout life—another example of where our hardwiring and environmental exposures collide to influence our behavior and preferences.

Taking Control of Your Own Sweetstat

My clinical observations hammer home the impact of highly sweetened drinks on appetite control and caloric intake. When people come into my office and tell me they are drinking eight liquids a day, four of which are sodas, three of which are specialty coffees, and one of which is a sports drink, I automatically ask them, "Where do you make room for plain, healthy water? How about milk?"

When I dig deeper into their thoughts and rationalizations, I hear, "Well, there's some milk in the coffee, and some water in the sports drink and sodas." So there is the "belief" that they are doing what is good for them and getting what they need, but in reality it is simply not so. What harm, if any, am I doing to my body, and by simply making better choices can I make a difference in my future health? They might be getting enough liquid from these beverages, but the important point is what else they are getting in the process.

When we are so busy feeding our sweet tooth, we deny our body's natural need for pure water and nutrient-rich milk. The "sweetification" of our food supply might be subtly resetting our sweetstat so that, like the boiling frog, we are all getting used to sweeter and sweeter things.

What I encourage is that you take control of your own sweetstat; put it on manual and shelter yourself from the seduction of increasing sweetification. Start slow, replacing just one of those sodas with water; that is the beginning of a decision to make a healthy choice. Even if society has temporarily dialed up your sweetstat, reset the dial and bring your taste expectations back down to a healthy level. This is a critical step to getting your binge eating and your eating in general under control, because insatiable desire for increasing sweetness can be an ongoing trigger for binges. By taking control of your sweetstat, you are in the driver's seat, not the food industry.

Our preference for sweets changes over our lifetime. Many adults might find Kool-Aid a bit hard to tolerate now but as children downed the stuff with gusto. I remember sucking down what was basically raw colored sugar from Pixy Stix as a staple of my childhood, but as an adult I much prefer dark chocolate with hazelnuts!

A glass of powdered fruit punch is sweet, no doubt, but is it sweeter than, say, a flavored coffee you picked up in a can at the 7-Eleven? Is it sweeter than that protein smoothie you had for breakfast, or for that matter, the flavored water you had at the gym after an otherwise great workout? What about the diet water, the sports drink, or the refined concentrated fruit juice you had for an afternoon snack to hold you over until you could drive to a coffee bar on the way home for a little afternoon mocha-latte-frappuccino-caramel pick-me-up?

Get to know what you drink, when you drink it, why you drink it, and how much of it you drink. The rest of this chapter details not only how to do that, but also how to remedy your choices if and when you decide to take control of your own sweetstat.

Record Your Habits in Your "Drink Diary"

You don't have to avoid sweets altogether. Sweets are pleasurable and play a role in our diet and our social world. Your main goal should be to be aware of the sweets you are eating and drinking and conscious of how they influence your self-control around food. We do not have to be passive victims of sweetification. With a little effort, we can gain awareness and control.

I believe that knowledge is power; knowing how many stealth sweets are contained in your beverages is a good place to begin slowly but surely eliminating them from your diet. Sweetened foods and drinks should be consumed consciously and in moderation, not routinely and without awareness of the sugar or noncaloric sweetener content. We often use food diaries with our patients, but more and more we are using "drink diaries," too.

In the past, when they self-monitored, many people didn't include what they drank, clouding the results of the food diary and confusing both patient and doctor as to why, when they were eating only twenty-five hundred calories a day they were gaining weight as if they were eating three thousand or more—or having afternoon or evening "sweet" cravings that couldn't otherwise be explained. But including the drinks they'd consumed in one day—in such things as flavored coffees, protein shakes, and power smoothies—revealed stealth sugars to be the source of the added calories and the cause of those sudden, unexplained cravings for more sweets after the drink was finished.

I had one patient who brought in her diary the first week and listed five coffees per day. Upon further questioning, it was revealed that to each of those coffees, she added two packets of Splenda and four packets of hazelnut nondairy creamer. She thought she was being calorie-wise by using the Splenda, but she failed to recognize that the nondairy creamer (which was available for free in her office break room) had five grams of sugar and forty calories per container. So in that little omission, we uncovered a five-times-per-day super-sweet infusion that also packed a whopping two hundred calories.

Begin a drink diary today. Remember, this is not so much about calories and pounds as it is about making you aware of the sugar, fat, and carbohydrates contained, stealthily, in some of our favorite drinks—drinks we down, without thought or concern of consequence, every day. Include water in your drink diary as well so you can work on increasing your water consumption at the same time. For instance, a page from a typical drink diary might look like this:

7 A.M.: Coffee with two creamers and one sugar

8:15 A.M.: Second cup of coffee; two powdered creamers and one Splenda packet

10:00 A.M.: Glass of water

10:30 A.M.: Power smoothie from cafeteria at work

12:15 P.M.: Iced tea with lunch/two sugars

3:22 P.M.: Diet soda

5:38 P.M.: Iced coffee with cream and sugar on way home

7:15 P.M.: Two glasses of red wine with dinner

8:00 P.M.: Glass of water

9:30 P.M.: Caffeine-free diet soda while watching TV

On the surface, this diary page looks okay so far, but to really become more conscious and aware of what we're recording, let's dissect this list to see what its author is actually consuming. In the table below, I break down the nutrient content into sugar/sweetening, carbohydrates, and fats in each of these drinks and give a daily total:

7 A.M.: Coffee with two creamers and one sugar
- Coffee—Sugar: 0; Sweetstat effect: low; Carbs: 0; Fat: 0
- Creamer—Sugar: 0; Sweetstat effect: medium; Carbs: 2 grams; Fat: 1 gram
- Sugar—Sugar: 4 grams; Sweetstat effect: high; Carbs: 4 grams; Fat: 0

8:15 A.M.: Second cup of coffee; two powdered creamers and one Splenda packet
- Coffee—Sugar: 0; Sweetstat effect: low; Carbs: 0; Fat: 0
- Creamer—Sugar: 0; Sweetstat effect: medium; Carbs: 2 grams; Fat: 0
- Splenda—Sugar: 0; Sweetstat effect: high; Carbs: 0; Fat: 0

10:00 A.M.: Glass of water
- Sugar: 0; Sweetstat effect: low; Carbs: 0; Fat: 0

10:30 A.M.: Power smoothie from cafeteria at work
- Sugar: 64 grams; Sweetstat effect: high; Carbs: 73 grams; Fat: 2.5 grams

12:15 P.M.: Iced tea with lunch/two sugars
- Tea—Sugar: 0; Sweetstat effect: low; Carbs: 0; Fat: 0
- Sugar—Sugar: 8 grams; Sweetstat effect: high; Carbs: 8 grams; Fat: 0

3:22 P.M.: Diet soda
- Sugar: 0; Sweetstat effect: high; Carbs: 0; Fat: 0

5:38 P.M.: Iced coffee with cream (2 Tbs) and sugar (4 tsp) on way home
- Coffee—Sugar: 0; Sweetstat effect: low; Carbs: 0; Fat: 0
- Sugar—Sugar: 17 grams; Sweetstat effect: high; Carbs: 16 grams; Fat: 0
- Cream—Sweetstat effect: medium; Carbs: 1 gram; Fat: 5 grams

7:15 P.M.: Two glasses of red wine with dinner
- Sugar: 0 grams; Sweetstat effect: medium; Carbs: 6 grams; Fat: 0

8:00 P.M.: Glass of water
- Sugar: 0; Sweetstat effect: low; Carbs: 0; Fat: 0

9:30 P.M.: Caffeine-free diet soda while watching TV
- Sugar: 0; Sweetstat effect: high; Carbs: 0; Fat: 0

All of the above information was collected, in one sitting, using various search engines, corporate and restaurant Web sites, and other online tools. For instance, I went to a famous fast-food company's Web site to find out the nutritional information for a packet of sugar, the manufacturer's Web site for the contents of a packet of nondairy coffee creamer, and the corporate Web site of my assistant's favorite smoothie company to find what's in her favorite afternoon treat.

Many companies literally had direct scans of the nutrition labels from their products posted online; others used helpful charts or other graphics that led me straight to the carbohydrate, sugar, and fat counts of all of the above beverage items. All of it was readily accessible and easy to understand. The total time I spent searching these sites was about half an hour. And, once *you've* done it a few times, it will just get easier and easier.

One last note: Interestingly enough, some of the columns that had the most zeros, such as packets of artificial sweetener or a diet soda, might have had the *lowest* calorie, fat, and actual sugar content but the *highest* sweetstat effect.

In short, the Internet provides you with plenty of resources to do this for yourself. Diagnose your own "drinking problem" so that you can figure out how best to get your liquid intake under control. Make sure you include both weekdays and weekends in your drink diary, because our drinking patterns often differ when we are on the job or in school versus on a day off.

After keeping a drink diary for a week you may find that you are basically a diet soft drink addict. I have one colleague who fits this description, and the thinking behind his addiction was fascinating. Although there were often ten to twelve empty plastic bottles under his desk by the end of the day, he rationalized his diet soft drink consumption by feeling good about recycling the bottles! Interestingly, once he kicked his diet soft drink habit, he also stopped binge eating alone in the kitchen at night.

Even if your daily beverage total of carbohydrates, fats, and sugars is zero, take a look at that sweetener column and see what is going on with your sweetness consumption. Even without the calories, you brain is experiencing the sweetness rush, and if presented with the choice of soda versus water, your brain will most likely have you reaching for the diet soda.

Codependent No More

Many of our drink choices are codependent; you buy a beverage and some little food item hitches a ride—chips to go with your soda, a few cookies with your milk, some pretzels or peanuts with your beer. This can be enough to unglue someone who is trying to get his or her urges to binge under control. For instance, Starbucks makes it easy for you to enjoy a scone or slice of biscotti with your mocha latte. Why, it's right there on the counter when you pay!

Just yesterday, I was in the airport buying a bottle of water to take on the plane. The person behind the counter asked me, "Would you like some chips or candy to go with that?" That salesperson probably wished she had never asked. I knew it was just her job, but I felt compelled to lecture her on the impact of her question on the obesity epidemic in general and on people with binge eating disorder in specific. She was glad to see me board that airplane. But maybe she learned something and fed it back to her boss.

So even when you are trying to do the right thing (buying

water), these "hitchhikers" can pop up unexpectedly and undermine your control. It's almost automatic these days, particularly because of the "do you want fries with that?" marketing at convenience stores, fast-food restaurants, and drive-throughs. The airport kiosk cashier made it sound like it was the most natural thing in the world to want some chips to go with my water.

The point is that not only are the extra sugar and extra sweetness appearing *in* your drinks, but they may also be showing up *as a result* of your drinks.

Pantry Raid!
Or, How to Do an Inedible Inventory

You can find out a lot about a person by simply snooping around his or her kitchen. Don't you know friends who have only natural, organic, or raw foods in their fridges? Who make their kids' lunches themselves and are home for dinner every night? Doesn't this tell you volumes about how they've chosen to live their lives, protect the environment, and even live longer?

What about your friends or family whose fridges and pantries look like the aisles of your local convenience store, filled with canned and bottled drinks, prepackaged foods, and take-out containers from this drive-through or that fast-food joint? Their kitchen stock reveals things about their personal lifestyle choices, too.

Your cupboards, cabinets, fridge, and pantry contain a valuable wealth of personal information you probably overlook on a daily basis. Don't overlook them anymore. Instead, do what I call a "pantry raid" and note the trends you spot.

This is an important personal inventory that will give you critical baseline data about you and your family. Start with the cupboards. Are they bare? Well stocked? Overflowing? What do you see? Many of us store our meal replacement shakes or protein powders here; still others store bottles of flavored, diet, or sweetened waters here. How many do you see? What brands? What do their labels promise? How often do you drink them?

Now let's move to the fridge. Open it up and peer inside. How many milk cartons are there? Juice containers? Sodas? Cans? Bottles? Glass? Plastic? Is there real food in your fridge, or just a vast wasteland of artificial, frozen, fast, and processed food? Are you spotting any trends yet?

Next stop: the pantry. By now you should be well aware of your current drinking habits and recognize recurring themes as the same containers or brand names keep showing up. Maybe you stock cases of your favorite meal replacement shakes right next to those convenient "fridge loader" soft drink containers; maybe you stocked up on gallons and gallons of sports drinks at a recent sale.

Final stop: overflow storage. Many people have an extra fridge or spillover pantry, a garage stockpile if you will, somewhere in the basement where they keep extras—like cases of soft drinks, alcohol, or other stockpiles of beverages and foods from the last run to your nearest members-only megamart warehouse, where things don't come in six- or twelve-packs but in cases, grosses, and lots.

What do *you* have in this second pantry? I have a vivid memory of my grandmother's stash of cherry pop, and my other grandmother's stash of Fresca! I didn't like either of them, but the garage and pantry were always stocked with their favorite drinks.

What has your tour taught you? What do you know now that you didn't, say, fifteen minutes ago? Have you taken note of some alarming patterns that are the domestic equivalent of finding ten to twelve empty plastic soda bottles beneath your desk at the end of every day? Or is family history perhaps repeating itself? Do you have your own silo of extra treats, snacks, goodies, and SSBs, just in case of "Appetite Armageddon"?

I'm not suggesting you dump out the contents of all those

sports drinks, flavored waters, meal replacement shakes, two-liter bottles, and soda cans. I am merely suggesting that knowledge is power; that knowing how many of these drinks—packed with stealth sugars and sweeteners—you drink a day tells you what your baseline is and what sort of changes you can make to start to take control on your next shopping trip or night out at a restaurant.

Be conscious of what you drink, how much, how often, and even when. What you learn could be just one more key to a successful recovery from binge eating disorder; but only if you take the time to do this self-inventory and really use it to your own benefit.

Remember that it is not always the big things we do once that count toward change, but the little things we do every day. The next time you shop or choose a drink, opt for something that doesn't have stealth sweeteners; maybe you'll choose it the next time, too. If you change a little now and a little more later, your big change comes in small doses—and just in time!

Be a "Sweet Sleuth"

When it comes to our lives, we often have our homes and then our "homes away from home"—work, your local coffee shop—second, third, and however many other places at which you spend a lot of time. Your primary home is a much more controlled environment than, say, your second, third, or fourth "homes."

At your primary home you are better able to keep track of exactly what you're drinking, the calorie count, the grams of sugar it contains. It's either all right there on the label or you're making it yourself; you're the one adding the ingredients controlling how much sugar you put in or leave out. Out in the world, in your second, third, and fourth places, others are in control.

Take work, for instance. Maybe the cafeteria makes your iced tea; maybe they have prepoured juice or a self-serve beverage dispenser. Either way, there are many more variables for how much sugar makes it into your drinks than back home, where *you* are in control. And it gets even more unclear in those third and fourth places where baristas make your coffee or teenagers pour your soda at a fast-food drive-through.

More and more, as we venture outside of our homes for additional eating and drinking choices, we are lulled into a sense of good health and goodwill by more and more companies claiming to offer heart-friendly fare or healthier alternatives to those "other" places. But as we've seen with one simple breakfast, what seems innocent on the outside can hide dozens of grams of stealth sugars—not to mention calories and fat—under its "healthy" banner.

Don't let too many sweets slip into your daily diet; be a "sweet sleuth" and detect the presence of such sweets on your own. Trust your taste buds to tell you when something is too sweet, not sweet enough, or just right. Be aware of hidden sweets on labels (see sidebar below), which is a great place to start your sleuthing.

Also restaurants—particularly the fast-food chains—are now listing not only the food on their menus but also its nutritional contents on their Web sites: Wendy's, Burger King, and McDonald's all do. More and more, sit-down chain restaurants like Applebee's and T.G.I. Friday's are printing the calories and fat grams contained in their menu items right on the menu.

This is progress; celebrate and take advantage of it!

But what about so-called healthier choices, like your local smoothie shop, "health food" store, or even the healthy aisle at your local grocery store? Don't assume that just because something says "healthy" or that the decor features autumn leaves and grapevines, all is well in the natural world.

Many a health food store contains foods that are packed with stealth sweets and artificially flavored beverages; talk to the people who work there and ask questions before you blindly make choices based on the healthiest-looking labels—or the promises on the packaging. Visit the corporate Web site and research before you buy. Trust your taste buds; if something tastes too good to be healthy, unfortunately, it might not be.

A colleague recently had a brief if intense flirtation with yogurt-covered raisins. Looking for a quick, convenient, and healthy afternoon snack, he discovered first vanilla and then chocolate yogurt-covered raisins and started munching on them instead of something less healthy from the vending machines down the hall. All was fine with the world until he compared

---

DECIPHER THE TERMS AS YOU READ THOSE LABELS

Marketers use a crafty set of code words to lure unsuspecting buyers into purchasing products that are less than healthy—and less than good for them. Don't be confused by labels that lull you into eating or drinking something that some clever marketer says will make you "feel" better for having chosen it. Here are some of the worst offenders—and what those taglines really mean:

- **Natural:** Don't be fooled by claims of "natural" on food labels; these days, such claims are a dime a dozen. In short, natural does not always mean "healthy." In the words of the USDA, "products that are 'natural' are not necessarily a healthy[ier] product. Fat in the marbling of a steak is certainly 'natural' but not considered a healthy source of protein."
- **All-natural:** Rarely are products bearing the all-natural label truly all-natural unless, that is, you planted, grew, farmed, and harvested them yourself! You may be able to

the nutrition label on his yogurt-covered raisins from the health food store and the label on a box of Raisinets he got at the movies—they were nearly identical! So much for health food. But such is the reason behind of the old adage: let the buyer beware!

You might be surprised to learn that the government is taking new and aggressive steps to inform consumers about the contents of their foods. In late 2006 the Food and Drug Administration (FDA) announced two new tools they were offering "to help consumers use the nutrition facts label to choose nutritious foods and achieve healthy weight management." These include "Make Your Calories Count," a Web-based learning program, and a new nutrition facts label brochure.[10]

Earlier that same year the FDA began insisting companies

get all-natural juice from a local grove or raw, unsalted organic nuts from a health food store, but in such cases many manufacturers can claim the end product is "all-natural" just because the source foods—nuts, fruits, etc.—were at one point all natural. This doesn't take into account various products added or taken out during the processing itself.

- **100% fruit juice:** Much like *all-natural*, 100 percent isn't quite what it used to be. For instance, a fruit juice may say that it contains 100 percent fruit juice. Then you may notice something else added, like sucrose or fructose— sugars *derived* from fruit sources. Therefore the juice is technically "natural" and "100%" fruit.
- **"Drink" versus "Juice":** When choosing between a processed juice drink or beverage don't grab the first thing you see; pay closer attention to make sure it's real juice not just another processed drink.

and manufacturers list "trans fat" on their nutrition labels. And even now comes word that new nutrition facts labels became a requirement in 2008, providing you with that much more information to add to your appetite arsenal; use it—and every other advantage you can gain from the simple acts of acquiring knowledge and doing your own research.

I'll never forget a colleague's tropical juice phase, during which he discovered a local "healthy" juice chain at a nearby shopping center. A few times a week, in between lunch and dinner, instead of a coffee drink or other pick-me-up, "Mark" would rave about his healthy juices and his zucchini, carrot, or walnut breads. He was almost obsessed with these healthful snacks—for about three weeks. Then I casually mentioned that he might want to visit the corporate Web site to find out just how many calories, carbs, and grams of sugar were in his strawberry banana juice or his beloved zucchini bread.

Once he did, Mark was shocked; his midday snacks were eating up huge chunks of his daily calories allowance: over 300 for the juice alone and another 450 for the zucchini bread! He was disappointed, so personally let down by the fact that this chain was touting these products as healthy, natural, and beneficial, when all along he'd been consuming a full third of his daily calories—not to mention dozens of grams of unwanted sugar—with each visit.

Mark's story highlights what so many of us experience when we rush headlong into this health phase or that, failing to heed our instincts and blindly trusting corporations to tell us what is good for us. Don't be fooled; be like Mark and do the research for yourself so you can make informed decisions.

The 1-2-1, H-2-o Solution

So how do I recommend solving this stealth sweetener and higher sweetstat dilemma? One word: water. Real water, pure water. Bottled or tap, it doesn't matter so long as it's not flavored or otherwise altered—i.e., not sweetened or colored, and with no added vitamins, starches, minerals, etc.

To get started, I recommend my 1-2-1, H-2-O Solution, which is quite simply this: For every sweetened beverage you drink each day, add another serving of water. For instance, if you have a cup of coffee with cream and sugar in the morning, great; but have a glass of water before you have a second cup. Enjoy that fountain soda on your way to work each morning? Fine; but have a glass of water when you get to the office. Have a glass of wine with dinner? Follow it with water.

In May of 2002 the *American Journal of Epidemiology* published research done at Loma Linda University in California. Researchers studied more than twenty thousand healthy men and women aged thirty-eight to hundred for six years. The study revealed that women and men who drank more than five glasses of water a day were significantly less likely to die from a heart attack during the study period than those who drank fewer than two glasses.[11]

Water has been praised throughout history as having a variety of healing, healthful, and restorative properties, including producing healthier skin, giving your body more energy, improving your digestion, reducing the amount and severity of headaches—the list could go on and on. More important, many patients with binge eating disorder, once they reteach themselves to like water, claim that it helps decrease their cravings for sweet foods and can even help them curb the urge to binge.

CHAPTER 7

Overcome Your Exercise Allergy (Reverse Your Activity Aversion and Move, Move, Move)

My top priority in life is my workout each day.

—JACK LaLANNE, AGE NINETY-THREE

Tish, whom you may remember from chapter 2, has been battling binge eating disorder for years, and she is now an example of someone who tends toward "too much of a good thing."

Take exercise; after triumphing over binge eating disorder, she needed someplace new to put her considerable energies. Exercise was her answer; the many hours she used to put into driving around looking for food for a binge, she now put into working out. I often tell Tish that even though she thought she had recovered from her eating disorder when she stopped binge eating, in reality she had just traded one obsession, binge eating, for another: exercise.

Tish worked out tirelessly; jogging, tennis, jazzercise, Pilates. Whatever the exercise fad was at the time, she tried it, loved it, mastered it, and maxed herself out doing it. Today Tish is recovering from rotator cuff surgery and feels miserable about sitting on the sidelines; she can't wait to heal and get back on the treadmill, StairMaster, or tennis court.

Many binge eaters engage in little to no physical movement, let alone formal exercise, during their disease and recovery. Others, like Tish, go to the opposite end of the spectrum during their recovery and overexercise. For the purposes of recovering from binge eating disorder, you should not focus on ultramarathons or extreme endurance challenges; aim for the happy medium where physical activity becomes an enjoyable part of your daily life—not some chore or an obsession. It should be a pleasant modicum of movement that is just right for you—and your mental and physical health.

Physical activity and true exercise can become a part of your daily life if you open yourself up to the challenge and the sheer physical and emotional joy of reveling in the beauty of movement. Physical activity (nonexercise activity) and formal exercise are critical to your health and well-being and you need strategies for increasing both of them. Uniting them is the concept of movement—movement can be anything from Feldenkrais to jogging.

The best way for you to think about adding more physical activity and formal exercise to your life is to think of physical activity as a gateway that leads to exercise. You start moving a little informally, maybe doing some routine gardening or even just household chores, and you get to like the feeling so much that you want to keep doing it. That's where formal exercise comes in.

Most important, whether you're just puttering around in the garden or lacing up for a five-mile jog, you need to unpack the thoughts associated with not being active and identify and break down the barriers that stand in the way of your getting a move on. I can give you a thousand reasons why you should increase your movement, but all of those reasons together won't be a powerful motivator unless you figure out what is standing in your way in the first place.

Are You "Allergic" to Exercise? Which Category Best Describes You?

Does the very thought of lacing up your sneakers or finding your gym membership card give you the cold sweats or a queasy stomach? Do your exercise-loving friends seem like members of an alien race?

According to the CDC, only "one-third of adults 18 years of age and over engage in regular leisure-time physical activity."[1] This despite the fact that, according to the Mayo Clinic, "The merits of exercise—from preventing chronic health conditions to boosting confidence and self-esteem—are hard to ignore."[2] But we are a country of people who know what we should be doing, even when we don't do it. We are the kings and queens of good intentions—even as we continue to be the international royalty of worldwide obesity.

To better understand your aversion to exercise, let's delve into the root of the problem. Read the following categories of exercise allergies to see where you belong:

- **The Treadmill Trauma Victim:** In elementary school, were you among the last to be chosen for a team? Remember the feeling of standing there while the captains were picking sides, knowing that you were going to be the last kid standing? Often our aversion to exercise arises in childhood, where athletic inability and/or insecurity about our weight, stamina, coordination, or looks is highlighted by the mob mentality and "only the strong survive" mantra that characterizes organized sports and physical education in most American schools.

- **The Lapsed Jock:** People who excel in sports during high school and college often lose interest in them as their adult years are taken up by "the real world," where work, relationships, bills, home ownership, shot knees, and stress often replace earlier, healthier habits. Your trophies might still be on the walls, but the size of your belly tells another story.

- **The "Blah" Factor:** Others lie somewhere in between the Treadmill Trauma Victim and the Lapsed Jock. They are neither scarred by bad exercise experiences in their youth nor reformed exercisers in adulthood; they are merely "blah" when it comes to exercise and can't quite get passionate about working out, walking, running, or even moving much.

- **The Prodigal Son (or Daughter):** Some people are just lucky, and genetics help them get through the first thirty years looking, if not exactly feeling, fit, trim, and slim. These people glide along for so long taking their trim waistlines for granted that they never quite realize that inactivity may catch up to them. Then one day they wake up to find their waistlines not so trim and themselves not so healthy.

Whichever category you fall into, or even if you fall into your own unique category, you need to work on your "exercise allergy"—and quickly. Fortunately, we've got a whole chapter to help you do that.

Start with Physical (Nonexercise) Activity

Liza is a receptionist for a law firm. She lives on the fifth floor in a two-bedroom apartment. Here's her typical day: She wakes up, goes to the kitchen, starts the coffeemaker, hits the microwave on button, eats, showers, takes the elevator to the garage, gets in her car, parks right outside of her place of work, takes the elevator to the eleventh floor where the offices are, gets the mail, and sits down immediately at her desk.

She stays at the desk until noon. If she needs to get something, she actually scoots her chair across her work space while she is still sitting in it. Her morning is answering phones, typing, and working at her computer. At noon, she takes the elevator down to the fifth-floor cafeteria, grabs a tray, and sits down for lunch. She takes the elevator back up, goes back to her desk and is there until five. After shutting down her computer she takes the elevator back down, gets into the car, drives home, takes the elevator up to her apartment, goes to the kitchen and turns on the TV there, and spends the night cooking, eating, watching TV, and sometimes bingeing.

As if preparing for hibernation, Liza appears to be on a "caloric expenditure conservation" program. She is barely expending any energy beyond her baseline resting metabolic rate. If she had a pedometer on, we'd be lucky to see the numbers go into the hundreds for any given day, let alone the thousands. The recommended number of steps for adult Americans is ten thousand per day! The convenience of her lifestyle is killing her.

As a scientist, I like data! In order to address your activity challenges, I want you to become an honorary scientist and embrace the numbers that can give you a baseline reading on your physical activity. The good news is that you don't need a degree or six more years of college; simply go out and buy a pedometer.

Pulitzer Prize–winning film critic Roger Ebert has lost a lot of weight using his pedometer over the last few years. Quoted recently in the *New York Times,* Ebert said, "I wear a pedometer, a little device that counts every step. It works as a goad, because you walk additional distances to pile up the numbers. The average person walks 2,000 to 3,000 steps a day. I walk 10,000 steps a day. I have lost a lot of weight as a result."[3]

These are simple, cheap little devices that count the number of steps you take during the day. Put it on and record your baseline steps in a day. For the best information do it on a typical weekday and a typical weekend day. Once you establish your baseline, you can start working toward incremental and attainable goals.

Overcoming Barriers to Exercise

Formal exercise feeds the body, the brain, the emotions, the job, the romance, the friendships, the bones, the blood, and the soul. It can keep you occupied during the tough times and make the good times better. It can increase your heart rate, blood flow, confidence, and even feelings of self-worth.

Many patients find that exercise is not only a great aid to therapy but also very therapeutic in and of itself. Exercise has been proven to elevate mood and alleviate stress; even just anticipating exercising (yes, I said anticipating exercise) can help elevate your mood. Exercise can also be an excellent way to bypass a binge not only because of its effect on appetite and mood but also because it gets you out of a bingeing situation. (It's pretty hard to binge eat on a treadmill in the gym.) So with all of these positive benefits, why do so few of us actually do it?

The toughest challenge in any healthy lifestyle program is getting people to make the active commitment to move their bodies *and* to stick with it. Let's face it: we're busy, time constrained, tired, and don't always like to sweat. Many of us seem almost averse to exercise, as if we are actually allergic to physical movement. As Erma Bombeck once said, "The only reason I would take up jogging is so that I could hear heavy breathing again."

Just the *e* word, *exercise*, can be a barrier—especially if you have a bad experience with exercise programs in the past, which many of us do. It can start as early as elementary school. Your recovery, however, is incomplete without the introduction of movement and exercise into your personalized recovery program.

It's funny how I have spent decades studying psychology, and the best advice I ever received wasn't from my professors or experts in the field, but from my relatives. My maternal grandfather—who was a great physical activity role model—used to say, "Energy breeds energy." I didn't really understand it at first, but it has since become my own personal mantra.

If I was feeling tired and lazy, he would often grab me, utter his famous phrase, and take me on a walk with him. Now this was no stroll in the park. He would take a tennis ball and bounce it while he was walking and we would talk about absolutely everything during those walks (which sometimes turned into five-mile hikes). He was right; I would come back refreshed and ready to tackle whatever tasks awaited me.

To this day if I am sitting in my office in front of my computer and my brain is fuzzy, I may think about getting a cup of coffee, but I hear my grandfather's words, and then slip my comfortable shoes on, bypass the coffee shop, and take a brisk ten-minute walk around campus. Then I come back and can focus; amazingly, without fail, my mind is always the better for the energy injection.

You've Got to Walk Before You Run:
Turning Physical Activity into Exercise

All physical activity is good. *All* movement is good. We need to move and move often, and for some of us that simply means moving more. But exercise does not have to be associated with a membership to a gym or even home-workout equipment, unless you count muscle shirts and sweat socks.

Many people don't exercise because they think they need special equipment or a personal trainer for it to qualify as exercise. But it doesn't have to be that way. We need to rethink how we define exercise, The Merriam-Webster dictionary describes exercise as the "bodily exertion for the sake of developing and maintaining physical fitness."

Exercise according to this definition can include a variety of physical movement—household chores, gardening, sports, play, recreation, etc. Of course, gardening a few times a week is good, but ultimately not enough; you want to spice up your movement with a variety of forms of exercise but also ensure that you exercise long enough and often enough.

To better understand how much and how often exercise is required, the fitness community has come up with something known as the FITT Method. FITT stands for:

- **Frequency:** how often you exercise (twice a day, twice a week, twice a month, etc.)
- **Intensity:** how much you challenge yourself when you exercise (slow pace, moderate pace, fast pace, etc.)
- **Type:** what specifically you do when you exercise (gardening, running, weight training, basketball, etc.)
- **Time:** how long you spend exercising (ten minutes, thirty minutes, sixty minutes, etc.)

Given these parameters, you can better gauge how beneficial your movement might be. For instance, when does a physical activity like gardening become formal exercise as dictated by the guidelines above? Well, here is where raw data come in handy. Case in point: gardening might not be enough movement—for a long enough time—to qualify as formal exercise if you have a postage-stamp-size lawn and can get out and weed only once or twice a week for twenty or thirty minutes at a time. Not only would you get bored quickly with that amount of activity but it also wouldn't do your body as much good unless you were adapting, monitoring, and growing in how you move throughout each week.

But if you have a fourteen-acre ranch and you are hacking down trees, mending fences, mowing the lawn, pulling up stumps, and tilling the soil four to five times a week for hours at a time, then gardening would qualify as exercise. (Sounds more like a full-time job, if you ask me.)

Either way, if it makes you sweat, moves your body, accelerates your heart rate, and makes you feel good, let's call it exercise. Want to get more specific? You're in luck. Guidelines for physical activity abound, including those developed by the American College of Sports Medicine (ACSM), the American Heart Association, and the august body of the Institute of Medicine (IOM).

A report was released from the IOM on the dietary reference intakes for energy, carbohydrates, fiber, fat, fatty acids, cholesterol, protein, and amino acids. This report recommended that all adults and children should participate in "60 minutes of moderate intensity exercise each day."[4] The report also recommended a dietary intake of 45 to 65 percent of calories from carbohydrates, 20 to 35 percent of calories from fat, and 10 to 35 percent of calories from protein.

The important thing is to start in your comfort zone of physical activity and then begin to expand that zone and challenge yourself with more traditional forms of formal exercise. As you continue to exercise and feel more comfortable, expand on the guidelines above and create your own. For instance, maybe sixty minutes of moderate intensity exercise each day won't be enough for you after moving your body for a few months; or you may need to split your sixty minutes up into two thirty-minute sessions—or, if you're chained to your desk all day, four sessions of fifteen minutes each.

I suggest you not follow a "paint-by-numbers" routine; instead, feel free enough with your body to color outside the lines and participate in those physical activities that you enjoy—and only as long as you enjoy them. There's no rule that says if you start your physical activity routine with jogging, you'll have to jog for the rest of your life; maybe you'll get into hiking or bicycling or playing tennis and enjoy that more. Maybe you will alternate your activities between walking on a treadmill during the winter months and hiking outdoors in the spring and summer. The choice is up to you; these are only guidelines to help you get started.

Something you like to do might also qualify as exercise if:

- **You sweat while doing it**
- **It increases your heart rate**
- **You have difficulty singing and doing it at the same time**
- **You can't do it in an evening gown or heels (with the exception of ballroom dancing!)**

I realize this can seem downright daunting if you've never exercised before or even if it's just been years since you fell off the treadmill. It's easy to hear how good exercise is for you and to know how to exercise; the hard part is simply getting up off the couch, lacing up your shoes, and getting out there and really doing it.

At this stage of your recovery from binge eating disorder, exercise is therapeutic.

When Cravings Strike, Strike Back—with Exercise

When cravings strike we can strike back—with exercise. Movement is the perfect antidote to cravings because it works on three separate levels:

- **Level 1—Physical:** You get up and out of wherever you are when the cravings hit. Once upon a time you might have run to the kitchen or the nearest convenience store or drive-through; now you can literally run around the block or to the nearest gym until the craving passes.

- **Level 2—Emotional:** Cravings are often less about hunger than they are about emotions; sometimes you may "feel" a craving the same way you sense other emotions, like fear, anger, happiness, and sadness. Well, in much the same way cravings are both physical and emotional, exercise also affects both the body and the mind. When you exercise you not only avoid the binge by physically doing something else but also assist your recovery by tackling the crave emotionally.

- **Level 3—Psychological:** Finally, when you battle a craving through movement you have a mastery experience. You can pat yourself on the back and say "job well done." When this happens often enough, these mastery experiences lead you to feel empowered to overcome your cravings, and your sense of empowerment (I *can* do this) increases. Your self-esteem increases, too, because you chose to take control over your eating via physical activity.

So when I talk about exercise I'm not just making some idle recommendation; It's a prescription—not a pill, not an ointment, but something you *have* to take to assist in your recovery.

The Gym Is Wherever You Hang Your Sweats

The ancient Greeks didn't have gym memberships or Stair-Masters, and they were the epitome of athletic prowess. They were followed by cultures where people received health benefits simply by working the land and eating what they grew. But now most of us work at sedentary jobs and buy our food. Gyms and home workout systems have replaced plowing fields and climbing mountains as our primary source of physical activity.

In this way, however, exercise has been automated the same way Ford automated automobile manufacturing and McDonald's automated mealtimes; we feel not just like we're on the treadmill but that we *are* the treadmill, going round and round without any real personal connection or, for that matter, motivation. If that's been your experience with exercise so far, wipe the slate clean and start over; today is a new day.

If you love your local gym or don't feel like you have enough discipline to start an exercise program on your own, go for it. This book is not antigym, but it *is* pro you.

Be realistic; know yourself before committing to something you know you won't stay with. If you positively, absolutely know that you'll never succeed in a gym, can't stand the thought of working out in front of other people, get grossed out by other people's sweat all over the machines, or just hate the concept of formal exercise in the first place, there is still hope.

The gym I want you to think about is portable, convenient, and affordable. Portable because you can wear it on your feet or tuck it under your arm; convenient because you can take it into your office, den, or backyard; and affordable because it can cost as little as the price of a new pair of running shoes or a yoga mat. You don't need to buy a lifetime membership to a gym.

Take a new look at the concept of the gym and adopt a new attitude concerning exercise. Realize that the new gym is anywhere you hang your sweats. It can be in your bedroom or your friend's garage; it can be jogging a few blocks around the neighborhood or walking on the beach.

Break down the barriers that have kept you from exercising and open yourself up to the idea that any moderate-intensity aerobic physical activity—as long as you do it long enough and often enough—can and should be considered exercise.

Best of all, you don't have to do the same activity every time. Below are two workout schedules from two vastly different patients. Read them both, then compare them to see which one is actually doing enough exercise each week.

PATIENT 1
Monday: Ran for 45 minutes
Tuesday: Cycled for 50 minutes
Wednesday: Ran for 45 minutes
Thursday: Off day
Friday: Ran for 45 minutes
Saturday: Cycled for 50 minutes
Sunday: Off day

PATIENT 2
Monday: Pilates 50 minutes
Tuesday: Gardened (weeded, tilled, mowed) for 40 minutes
Wednesday: Off day
Thursday: Cleaned out garage for 2 hours
Friday: Off day
Saturday: Off day
Sunday: Bicycled with friends for over 2 hours

The answer is both of the above. Patient 1 is clearly engaging in moderate-intensity aerobic physical activity for a minimum of thirty minutes five days each week or vigorous-intensity aerobic activity for a minimum of twenty minutes three days each week. Patient 2 is less of an exerciser, but is definitely approaching that goal of thirty minutes per day on average.

Sure, maybe the patient who jogs at the same time, for the same duration, at the same level of intensity five days a week is exercising more often, but look again at the guidelines from the American College of Sports Medicine and the American Heart Association. Doing vigorous exercise for as little as twenty minutes three days a week is as beneficial as working out moderately five times a week. So our gardener/garage cleaner/bicyclist is exercising effectively.

Two Is Company; Three's Allowed

For some of us, exercise is a solitary pursuit. We love the peaceful ebb and flow of a quiet morning jog alone or we can't wait to queue up our favorite tunes on our iPods and hit the elliptical trainer before anyone else is even awake. Our early-morning or evening workouts are often the only times we have that solitude.

Others need a little help getting motivated or simply want an excuse to include their friends as they launch their new physically active lifestyle. Some people find that when they are not distracted by others they focus on the negative aspects of what they are feeling during exercise ("my legs are tired," "I'm really too stressed to run," "I felt a little twinge in my knee," etc.) and that makes it more likely that they will cut their workout short. Having someone to distract you from your internal chatter can keep you from making mental mountains out of physical molehills. If you're engaged in lively conversation, you might not even notice that transient twinge.

There are advantages to exercising with someone else. For instance, people who exercise together have a second, third, or even fourth or fifth pair of eyes checking out that alarm clock in the morning or stopwatch in the afternoon; that means fewer missed opportunities for exercise and twice the motivation to get up and get out there.

For those of us who find it monotonous to exercise, the com-

THINK OUT OF THE BOX (OR OUT OF THE GYM)

Many people get stuck in trying to develop a physical activity or exercise plan because they limit their choices to the same old activities, such as jogging, walking, aerobics, and swimming. In developing your plan, it's great fun to think completely out of the box and to try activities that you have no experience with. It can be both exhilarating and humbling to try a new activity as an adult. As long as you keep your sense of humor, it can also be a lot of fun. Here are some things that my patients and friends have reported trying:

- **T'ai chi** originated in China and is a form of martial arts. It is practiced around the world often by groups of people outdoors in the morning. T'ai chi is associated with health benefits and stress reduction.
- **Ballroom dancing** is a mixture of physical activity and a social event. Many studios around the country do not require you to sign up with a partner and have lessons for all ages. In fact, you can even indulge your adventurous spirit by trying salsa, swing dancing, tango, or hip hop. Find a beginners' class and give it a whirl.
- **Yoga** originated in India but has become a popular form of mindful physical activity around the world. Yoga makes the body strong and flexible and brings about clarity of mind.

pany of friends, family, or even new acquaintances can eliminate that boredom; many people who exercise together claim
the time flies by and they can exercise twice as long together as
they could alone.

If exercising with a partner or a group sounds like it might
be just the thing for you, here are some great tips for making
the most out of joint workouts.

- **Cultural and ethnic dancing** can be wonderful exercise
  and a great way to meet new people, regardless of your
  ethnicity and background. Whether you decide to try
  Irish step dancing, belly dancing, African dance, square
  dancing, flamenco, salsa, or any other variety of dance,
  you will find it an enlightening experience.
- **Water wellness** is an excellent alternative to traditional
  exercise, especially if you have trouble with your joints. If
  you belong to a pool or have one nearby, encourage the
  management to develop water-based exercise programs,
  if they don't already exist.
- **Feldenkrais** is a way of working with the awareness of
  your body to improve its range of motion and function.
- **Roller skiing** is for the truly adventurous, but in Scandi-
  navia, at least, age is no barrier to enjoying this non-
  snow equivalent of cross-country skiing. In the United
  States, we are starting to see more of roller skiing,
  which is a great aerobic activity that is sure to turn some
  heads.

Whatever you decide to try, be brave. Make sure your doctor is
on board with your trying a new activity and leave your shyness
at home. The important thing is to move, move, move.

- **More people, more variety:** When left to our own devices, we'll often do the same thing over and over again. Maybe jogging is the easiest, push-ups are the most familiar, or shooting baskets by ourselves is the only thing we can fit in at the end of the day. When we work out with a partner, we can play off each other by always suggesting something new to do. Tennis one day, volleyball the next, a walk around the mall on Thursdays, and hiking every Saturday. Take advantage of the joint atmosphere and use it to make every day a new day.

- **Round robin:** Merely getting up to exercise can be the biggest obstacle for some of us with exercise allergies, but you can eliminate the need for an alarm clock by doing a "round robin" with your friends instead. Have them call you at a certain time; then you call the next person and that person calls the next. Greet each person with a motivating message, and by the time you all meet up, you might just be looking forward to exercise. (And even if you're not, the extra motivation never hurts!)

- **Accountability counts:** We all have valid reasons for not exercising: work commitments, getting sick, even aches and pains from overexercising! But when is an excuse valid and when is it just an excuse? Friends and family can help you answer this question, but more important, help you avoid making excuses by holding you accountable for your actions. When you are part of a group that exercises together, every time you're not there the group is affected; for some of us, this can be reason enough to get out of bed and out into the world to exercise.

- **A little competition never hurts:** And if you happen to have a competitive streak, having others around just might bring out the best in you. "Hey, if she can lift twenty-five pounds, I can too. Maybe even thirty!"

Here are some popular forms of exercise you can do alone or with friends, co-workers, and family:

1. **Do the mall walk:** If the gym isn't your scene and an idyllic run alone around the neighborhood is your own personal nightmare, join your friends and take to the mall. Many local malls encourage people to walk their corridors in the morning, providing a safe, controlled, clean environment where groups of three, four, five, or six can stroll at their own pace and get in quite a workout—if they don't stop to shop at every other store! One advantage to these morning walks is that the food courts often aren't open that early, so you can experience being in a mall and not eating!

2. **Back to the playground:** How long has it been since you played basketball or four square, used a hula hoop, or even jumped rope? Why let the kids all have the fun? Scout out your neighborhood or a five- to ten-mile radius for the nearest playground, ballpark, or recreation center and then use it. This can help you add variety to your workout routines and also give you more choices when boredom inevitably sets in. It can also remind you that activity is fun!

3. **Do your chores:** Go help someone move one afternoon and then tell me you didn't burn a few hundred calories and double your heart rate in the process. Gardening, renovating your house, cleaning out your garage, mowing the lawn—these can all be great sources of exercise and movement as well as super ways to get brownie points from your spouse or kids!

4. **We'll do lunch—in the parking lot:** A common excuse for those allergic to exercise is the time-honored "I'm too busy to exercise before (or after) work." Well, when you can fit in a little exercise *at* work, no more excuses, right? Many employees walk the perimeter of the employee parking lot during lunch and breaks, often with co-workers, to break up the monotony and add to the camaraderie of workplace exercise. Not only is it a great way to bond with fellow employees, but it's a super way to get your exercise in without having to do it before *or* after work. Don't have the right shoes? That's no excuse. Keep an old pair of running shoes or flats under your desk to slip on when you make your escape.

5. **Embrace the weekend:** Spend the weekend exercising. That doesn't give you the week off, of course, but I do find that many of my patients have twice as much time—and twice the energy—on the weekends to find new and inventive ways of exercising. This does not mean you should go hog wild on the weekends to the point of injuring yourself so you *can't* be active during the week. Ramp up the weekend exercise but don't overdo it in the process.

Everything in Moderation

Take it slow. I want you to get excited about exercise as you've never gotten excited about anything else in your life—but not to the point of exhaustion or injury. There's nothing worse than having your best laid plans for lifestyle change interrupted because you did too much too soon and got injured. That can lead straight to unhealthy cognitions: "I've never been any good at sports, forget this; I may as well just give it up and binge." Sure, there may be some soreness and even aches and pains, particularly if you've never formally exercised before, but you can navigate those pitfalls by listening to your body and knowing when to say when.

One of my colleagues recognized that she needed to heed the advice that she was giving to our patients and decided to start running (for the first time ever). She started with a friend who had *no* appreciation of what it felt like to run if you have never run before and are totally out of shape. His belief was that "anyone could run a mile." So she went out for her first run and started having that burning pain in her lungs, thick saliva in her mouth, and a face as red as a beet.

His solution was "just run through it." She tried that twice and thought she was going to die. So she called me up and said, "This hurts so much, I'm going to quit." When she told me her friend's advice, I understood the problem and gave her my advice, which was completely the opposite. In those early stages, mark off a mile loop. Walk a little bit first to get loosened up, then start running slowly. When it gets uncomfortable, ratchet it down to a brisk walk and breathe deeply. Then when you feel stronger again run a little more.

Over time, using this more realistic and incremental approach, you'll find that you can go longer and longer without breaks and then maybe even want to go longer than a mile. This way you can ease into it without the misery and without the intense urge to give up. My colleague can now include two-mile runs in her weekly routine. Every once in a while she still may slow down in the middle of a run if she hurts or is tired or is emotionally drained, but she keeps walking—and *that's* movement!

The beautiful thing about exercise is that it's a lifelong endeavor; no need to rush or overdo it. Sometimes we can take it to extremes. Know your limits and heed them well. A little soreness in your knee is one thing, but if it becomes painful to keep jogging or walking or playing tennis or shooting hoops, stop. Exercise is supposed to help your body, not damage it. When you truly start to hit your stride and include movement, activity, and yes, even formal exercise into your daily routine, you will finally know what everyone else who exercises has known all along: It's a really great feeling.

CHAPTER 8

Embrace Technology as Therapy

The advance of technology is based on making it fit in so that you don't really even notice it, so it's part of everyday life.

—BILL GATES

Technology has become both a blessing and a curse. First the radio, then TV, then computers for work, then the Internet, now blogs and video games and cell phones and PDAs and Segway scooters and motorized bicycles and massage chairs—all have contributed to our sedentary way of life. Frank Booth, Ph.D., has coined the term Sedentary Death Syndrome, or SeDS, to describe the potential link between a sedentary (or physically inactive) lifestyle and a host of preventable diseases such as high blood pressure and heart attacks, type 2 diabetes, and breast and colon cancer.

Rather than criticizing technology for contributing to sedentary behavior, I figure it's here to stay, so we may as well figure out a way to make the most of it—in this case, by using it to control binges and *decrease* sedentary behavior. Our computers, workstations, PDAs, and cell phones can be our allies in recovery from binge eating disorder.

Self-Monitoring:
The Key to Recovery

Every technological tool in this chapter can aid you in self-monitoring—keeping track to see if you're reaching your daily, weekly, and monthly goals along the path to recovery. Self-monitoring is the best predictor of behavior change.

At the UNC Eating Disorders Program, when we ask patients to self-monitor, we encourage them to do things like keep a food log; catalogue cravings; make shopping lists, to-do lists, and journals; keep appointments; join support groups; and the like. The more you monitor yourself, the more you become aware of your patterns, habits, red flags, and danger signals. For instance, by keeping track of the times, places, and situations when you crave food the most—e.g., noticing that you are impossibly hungry at four in the afternoon or four in the morning, for example—we can more accurately pinpoint these periods as danger zones and better avoid them in the future.

Self-monitoring seems like such a simple thing, and yet for many people it actually becomes quite challenging. They start off strong during the first few weeks of recovery; they stick to schedules, make their appointments, buy their fresh veggies, get up and get out for movement, pre-prepare their meals to make breakfast a priority, and then, either gradually or all of a sudden, they stop.

We recently had a group of patients here at UNC beg us to create a "graduate" program to follow their original eight-week weight-loss curriculum in order to help them stay on top of the skills they learned, including their self-monitoring. We asked what we could do to ensure that they kept coming back for the graduate program. Nearly unanimously, they said that the surefire method for getting them to come back would be to make them pay in advance. So we took their advice and asked for prepayment, but after about two weeks, attendance started dwindling and the majority of the class stopped showing up!

They truly thought that prepaying would be enough to get them back, but once the official class was over, other things took priority. They still desperately want this support, but this experience taught us that we need to find ways—probably technological ones—to bring the support to them.

Up until now, maybe you have been trying to keep track of your urges to binge using tried-and-true (but boring and outdated) pencil and paper techniques. The number of times I have heard "the dog ate it" or "I left it in the car" or "I did the first two days, then gave up" or "I was afraid someone would see it" makes it painfully clear to me that paper and pencil self-monitoring is not the favorite pastime of most people.

Using technology to help you self-monitor seems to be less associated with drudgery, boredom, or embarrassment than the standard paper-and-pencil diary and can become a valuable asset to your recovery.

Don't Forget to Set the Alarm

Most of us take an alarm clock for granted, but it can literally create more time for you to assist in your recovery. How? Let's say you start using a pedometer to help you keep track of how many steps you take each day. However, at the end of each day you find that you're just not reaching your goal. By setting your alarm clock fifteen minutes earlier you can use that time to take a quick walk—or two—around the block and reach your daily goal.

Or what if you're not keeping up with your daily food logs, online journal, or various resource activities prescribed by your counselor? If work or school is too hectic, lunch is too rushed, and the evenings tend to get away from you, set your alarm clock to give yourself fifteen or twenty minutes a day for updating all your paperwork.

And don't just think of "alarm clock" as the digital device you have next to your bed. Did you know that most watches come with an alarm clock feature, as do most cell phones and desktop and laptop computers?

Make Your PDA Your BFF

Depending on the sophistication level, price, and model of your PDA, you will likely have a variety of the following features included in your basic model: alarm feature, calendar, e-mail, voice mail, voice recorder, phone capabilities, and basic organizational tools such as those designed to let you create to-do lists and reminders, and even manage spreadsheets and basic text documents.

Schedule self-monitoring time or walk time or take-a-trip-up-the-stairs time using your calendar function and have your PDA beep you at appropriate increments throughout the day. You check your screen, it says "self-monitor" or "hit the stairs," and you have a personal reminder to engage in the behavior you truly want to do.

Also, in most PDAs there is a "repeat appointment" function. You have to type it in only once and it will remind you every day at the same time. People who have to take medicines on a regular schedule have known about effectively using this for years. By using your alarm clock throughout the day—not just in the morning—you can remind yourself of when it's time to do something you should be doing to aid in your recovery, and give yourself more time in which to do it.

Even the most basic PDA capabilities can be enlisted to provide essential functions in your recovery from binge eating disorder:

- **Alarm feature:** Remind yourself of various recovery duties throughout the day—not just in the morning—with your PDA's alarm feature. This could include settings to remind you to eat breakfast at a certain hour (so you don't skip it) and of lunchtime, snack time(s), and dinnertime. You could also remind yourself when to go to the gym, meet with your counselor, attend a class or session, write in your journal, or read a blog.

- **Calendar:** When you have a built-in feature like a PDA calendar, you can mark down what days you go to the gym, when you grocery shop, what days you have to attend classes and/or sessions and various social functions relating to your recovery, and a host of other recovery-related reminders.

- **E-mail:** Keep in touch with your friends, family, and support group(s) with your PDA's e-mail feature. Or e-mail yourself news stories, alerts, and/or reminders throughout the day.

- **Voice mail and/or voice recorder:** If you're an auditory learner, leave yourself a voice mail and/or use your PDA's voice recorder option to leave messages for yourself throughout the day. The messages can range from the mundane, like "Remember to pick up vegetables on the way home from work tonight" to the empowering: "Don't let that lost promotion get you down; remember that you're almost through with that night course and can reapply again at the end of this quarter."

- **Phone capabilities:** With your PDA, you can always be one quick phone call away from a friend, family member, or supporter in your times of need. Say you're having an irrational craving at three in the afternoon; a quick call to someone who understands can help walk you through it until you're okay to navigate the treacherous waters of snack time by yourself. Often, by the time you're done with the call—this works with e-mail and text features as well—you will have managed to outlast the craving and it's already long gone.

- **Texting:** We'll speak more about this a little later in the chapter, but for now know that texting yourself and others is a great way to stay on track with your recovery.

- **To-do lists:** "Buy fresh veggies @ stand on corner." "Meet with support group after church." "Pick up healthy snacks." "Renew gym membership." "Finish reading chapter 7 of *Crave*." These are just several popular examples of how to-do lists can help make your recovery an easier one—and your PDA a lifesaver.

- **Reminders:** The reminder feature on your PDA, combined with your to-do list and calendar features, can all work in conjunction to leave you no excuses for the recovery activities you need to perform throughout the day. For instance, we all know repetition is the key to success. So if you add to your calendar that Monday you're due for a Pilates class at the gym, then key it into your to-do list *and* schedule it for an automatic reminder at, say, noon the day of. Now your chances of missing this important date are next to nil.

- **Spreadsheets and basic text documents:** Use the spreadsheet and basic text document features of your PDA for longer documents, such as shopping lists, journal entries, and names and addresses of various support groups.

Walk Your Way to Recovery with Your Pedometer

Buy yourself a pedometer—that handy, portable little counting device that adds up the steps you take each day. They're cheap, so buy one for each member of your family. How many pedometer steps each day is enough? In an article for *Sports Medicine* journal, Dr. Catrine Tudor-Locke asserts that to classify someone as active they should achieve ten thousand steps per day.[1]

Most people I know don't even come close to that. So let's use these simple little gadgets to challenge ourselves to reach some activity goals. Here's a three-step plan to help you do that:

1. **First establish your baseline.** Wear the pedometer for a typical weekday and a typical weekend day. *Don't change anything about your behavior.* Find out what the typical number of steps you take each day is. Now, you can't wear your pedometer in the pool, and it won't tally up activities like cycling, but it is a good approximation of how active you are.

2. **Once you have your baseline, set a reasonable first goal.** Maybe aim for a thousand steps above your baseline. Remember, ten thousand is the ultimate goal, but if you try to set your first goal at that when your baseline is two thousand, you'll be setting yourself up for failure! So let's imagine that your baseline is three thousand steps. Your first goal is going to be a full week where five out of seven days you reach four thousand steps.

3. **Keep setting goals in natural increments.** Next, reward yourself, not with food, but maybe with a walk in a nice neighborhood or window shopping or a yoga

class. Then up your goal by another thousand and aim for the same thing—five out of seven days reaching five thousand. Do this until you reach the ultimate goal of ten thousand steps per day if you can. But if you truly can't get there, every level up is a step in the right direction.

Here are just a few more simple ways to let your pedometer help you reenergize your life by keeping track of how many steps you take each day.

- **Don't let the day get away from you:** If you find yourself too many steps away from your goal at the end of each day, be more diligent about apportioning them throughout the day so that you don't face the majority of your steps after you're already pooped. Does this advice sound familiar? Like spreading your caloric intake across the day? I know time is of the essence for us all, but remember the alarm clock tips from the previous section to get up a little earlier to get your walk in. Walk to work, if possible, or get off the bus, train, or subway two or three stops before yours or park a little farther away to get more steps in getting to the office. Walk during your breaks and at lunchtime, or right after work so you're not left staring at those missing few thousand steps at the very end of the day.

- **Buddy up:** If you know you're the kind of person who will not achieve your goal to walk more steps each day if you try to go it alone, buy two pedometers instead of one. Give the extra to a friend, family member, classmate, or co-worker and urge them to help you stay on schedule by walking with you one to two times per day or during the week. When it comes to a successful recovery, it could just be the cheapest investment you ever make.

- **Benchmark yourself off the bench:** The best way to make sure you're reaching your goals when it comes to walking enough each day is to give yourself benchmarks. These could be as simple as "two thousand steps before breakfast" or "a thousand steps during lunch," but each benchmark serves a purpose, because the more you have, the less likely you are to wind up a few steps shy of your daily goal each night.

- **"Walk with the Lord":** One of my favorite stories comes from a colleague's patient who had been having a hard time finding a walking partner. She came in one day thrilled and said, "Doctor, I found myself the most reliable walking partner." When my colleague asked for details she replied, "I am walking with the Lord!" This resourceful woman had paired up her daily prayers with her daily walk and felt sure the Lord would be supportive of this particular type of multitasking. For those of you less religiously inclined, it can also be a time to sort through your thoughts, think about the ones you love, or search for a little more balance or nature in your life.

Let Your Fingers Do the Talking:
Text Your Way Back to Health

What better way to put your cell phone to use than to keep in touch with your support group of friends, family, counselors, doctors, and fellow binge eaters by texting words of encouragement and support, or even helpful reminders—"did you remember to eat breakfast today?"

Many people find that organizing themselves is a big challenge in their busy, daily lives. But don't overlook the obvious when scouting for ways to remind yourself when to eat, how much to eat, what you need to eat to be healthy, or even when a friend is available to help you through a tough craving time.

Here are some great tips for using texting to keep your recovery on track.

- **Reach out for support:** One of the greatest advantages of modern technology is being able to reach almost anyone, at any time, anywhere. This is particularly important to someone recovering from binge eating disorder, who needs support from friends and family. When you find yourself backsliding into old behaviors or getting tempted to succumb to familiar cravings, reach out for support—and fast—with a short text message to someone you know will get right back to you.

- **Knowledge on the go:** A little knowledge can go a long way, and the right knowledge can be priceless. Texting is perfect for exchanging topical headlines, facts, statistics, quotes, and even links to help further your recovery with up-to-the-second information from trusted sources.

- **Words of encouragement:** I have found that the right words at just the right time often make the difference between a good day and a bad one. Get in the habit of collecting cell phone numbers of those in your circle of support, and text one another regularly as you run across—or think of—kind, thoughtful, prophetic, or helpful words. Giving is often as good as receiving, and you never know when the words *you* send could just make the difference in someone else's recovery program.

- **Helpful reminders:** I like to recommend that patients enter into a "circle of three" to help keep them on the right track during the initial stages of recovery and, for some, to prevent relapse. This circle of three includes any three friends, family members, co-workers, classmates, or fellow patients who regularly check in with each other throughout the course of the day. For instance, when two of your circle of three know that you have a big presentation coming up that you are nervous about, and is likely to be a binge trigger, they can fling you a text message of support to help you get through the tense times.

Connecting with Yourself and Others
Via the Internet

Our parents used to call doctors or their nurses for information about illnesses and treatment, but the Internet has replaced the family physician as the number one place that people turn for health-care information. As with everything, there is both good and bad information on the Internet about binge eating disorder.

We and other groups have been actively involved in using the Internet to get resources for treatment and prevention of eating disorders to people. In fact, a recent study reported that "an Internet-based program may help prevent eating disorders in college-aged women who are most at risk." Researchers responsible for the study, which was first reported in the August 2006 issue of the *Archives of General Psychiatry*, recruited nearly five hundred college-age women from the San Diego and San Francisco Bay areas who were "at risk for developing eating disorders."[2]

Funded by the National Institute of Mental Health, the study set up an online resource program called "Student Bodies" to help "reduce young women's concerns about their weight and body image." Women who participated in the Student Bodies program were expected to read and complete weekly online assignments, participate in online discussion groups and self-monitoring, and/or write entries in a journal for an eight-week period.

Explains lead author of the study Dr. C. Barr Taylor of Stanford University in California, "This is the first study to show that eating disorders can be prevented among high-risk groups . . . I suppose the most important message is that eating disorders can be prevented . . . Internet-based prevention interventions can be effective and reach large populations at relatively low cost."

The great thing about finding support on the Internet is that it is a place where most of us already spend an inordinate amount of time every day. I recognize that time is at a premium these days, so when I can suggest using a tool we're already familiar with to help in recovery, I am talking about using the time—or a small portion of it—you already spend on the Internet to help you recover, and in a more long-lasting manner.

There are a variety of online ways to get help for your recovery from binge eating disorder.

- **Information:** Knowledge is power, and the more you know about binge eating disorder and the help you can find online, the more chances you'll have to recover from this serious illness. Information is everywhere on the Internet. Just be sure that what you are finding comes from credible sources like universities, recognized journals, accredited foundations, or nationally recognized organizations. (A list of such places can be found in chapter 9.)

- **Support:** One sure way to assist your recovery is to surround yourself with helpful, resourceful people who already know what you're going through. Even if you never meet these people, online support groups can often be helpful in your times of need. Again, research the group thoroughly before entering and be wary of giving out too much personal information online. Safe Internet practices apply here, as they do everywhere on the Web.

- **Comfort:** Reading about others who've gone through an eating disorder and recovered can often be an inspiring and helpful way to assist in your own recovery. Resources like amazon.com can offer you dozens of such stories in the form of gripping memoirs and self-help books. If cost is an issue, start a "book of the month" club among your support group and share books periodically throughout the year.

Blog Your Way to Bliss

Before Valerie Bertinelli lost forty pounds, wrote a book, and went on the talk-show circuit to inspire millions of others, she was an official blogger for Jenny Craig weight loss systems. By chronicling each week of her progress, Valerie helped both herself and others through the good times and the bad times associated with any weight-loss regimen.

As Valerie's success story shows, the written word can be a powerful healing tool, particularly when you're writing your own story. Many people find that chronicling their experience of recovery in one way or another brings them clarity and shared support, compassion, and understanding. More and more they are choosing to take their thoughts, emotions, and stories online to blog about the experience.

Blogging, otherwise known as electronic journaling, can turn tears into triumph by systematically bringing your struggles to life in a way that makes them both real and, as a result, conquerable. When you write about your problems you make them authentic; when they are authentic, you can no longer hide from them and they, in turn, become things you have to deal with.

I have read many eloquent blogs by my patients and am always touched by how freely they express their emotions electronically—sometimes more so than in face-to-face therapy. This is one of the major reasons I recommend chronicling your recovery and, for the technologically savvy, blogging. Here you can reveal your deepest emotions and choose who gets to read about them. But most important, you can get support.

When people comment on your blog you can feel a true community of sharing and support. Maybe this is what women used to do when they held quilting bees on Friday evenings. I don't know about you, but I haven't been to a quilting bee in a long time (ever, in fact). More power to those of you out there who have, but we are social animals and we need the support of others! Blogging is a great way to get that support during your recovery.

Many blogging sites are public, and personally, I recommend you avoid those at this time. For now, blog for yourself and a select chosen few whom you invite—or who ask to be invited into the fold. This allows you to control who is and how many are reading your life story. It also gives you the freedom to speak openly about your problems and exchange ideas with your readers about how to help one another. As you progress and grow throughout your recovery, you can consider whether to open your story up to a wider audience. That is an entirely personal decision. After all, you never know who might be so affected by your words that they seek recovery themselves.

CHAPTER 9

One Size Doesn't Fit All, or Why Not All Treatments Are Equal

A central focus of National Institute of Mental Health (NIMH) treatment research has been finding a more tailored, individual approach to therapy.[1]
—THOMAS R. INSEL, M.D., DIRECTOR, NIMH

When it comes to treatment, some health care professionals can become a little dogmatic about their particular approach and think it's the best fit for everyone. I can't necessarily blame them. I mean, if you found something that not only worked for you but dozens, maybe even hundreds, of others, wouldn't *you* want to shout it from the rooftops?

My approach is a little different. I want you to do what works for you, period. If that means one particular treatment, to the exclusion of all others, great. But if that means sampling from a variety of treatments and taking a little of what works from each, then so be it. In other words, if you really give this one particular approach a good, hard try and it still hasn't curbed your binge eating, then it makes perfect sense to look for other approaches that either on their own or together with this approach work for you.

I believe that if there is just one person out there for whom an approach is effective, that approach deserves to be viewed as a valid and credible treatment option (unless utter quackery is involved).

There are many reasons why a particular approach might work for some and not work for others. I believe that timing is a big issue when it comes to treatment. After all, just because something may not work for you now doesn't mean that it will not be the right fit for you at a later date. Some people might find a more flexible treatment program helpful in their youth, but as they get older find that there is comfort in greater discipline. It is all about finding the right fit at the right time.

Ever wake up one morning to the news that a certain diet is suddenly all the rage? I remember the day I first heard about the seaweed diet. Nearly a dozen people were talking about it at work one particular Monday. Treatments—like diets, fashion designers, and movie stars—do come in and out of vogue for one reason or another, but it is wise to take a long hard look at the ones that have staying power. I suppose it's human nature to want to jump on the bandwagon of something new—or even old—if it suddenly seems like it's working for everyone you know. I always tell patients to make rational decisions and to start with treatments that have a basis in science, regardless of what's most fashionable at the time.

As we have been discussing, the goals for the treatment of binge eating disorder are twofold: to reduce and preferably eliminate eating binges and, when necessary, to lose and ultimately maintain a healthy weight. But generally speaking, that is not enough. Because binge eating is so intertwined with shame, poor self-image, self-disgust, and other negative emotions, treatment also needs to address associated psychological issues. This comprehensive approach is essential for long-term recovery. Good, clinically tested treatment and early intervention can make a world of difference.

In 2006 my team at UNC completed a government-sponsored review of *all available treatments* for binge eating disorder in order to see if we could draw any firm conclusions about what treatments are the most effective.[2,3] We looked at psychotherapy, medication, behavioral weight-loss programs, nutrition education, self-help approaches, and twelve-step programs. At the time there were twenty studies available in the literature that were of a high enough quality to be reviewed in our report. Here's what we discovered.

Psychotherapy

We reviewed all psychotherapy studies. Psychotherapy, whether in individual or group sessions, can help teach people how to exchange unhealthy habits for healthy ones and reduce bingeing episodes. It teaches how to monitor eating and moods, develop problem-solving skills, and respond to stressful situations. Psychotherapy can also help improve mood and relationships.

Our results showed that one type of psychotherapy in particular was effective, namely cognitive behavioral therapy, or CBT. Many of the techniques you have learned in this book fall under the heading of CBT. Basically, the principles behind CBT are to identify unhealthy thoughts that may fuel binge eating behavior and replace them with healthier ones that support healthy behaviors.

For example, an unhealthy thought such as "I know I have no self-control, why should I even pretend that I can curb this crave?" is likely to be a self-fulfilling prophecy and ultimately lead to one whopper of an all-or-nothing binge. But learning to use that unhealthy thought as a warning signal for change, and transforming that thought into a healthier alternative such as "Okay, this has been a high-risk situation for me in the past, but I have some new skills I can put to use to try to curb this crave!" increases your odds of having a successful outcome and avoiding that binge in the first place. It all begins with being mindful, or aware of your thoughts and the power that your thoughts have to influence your behavior.

Overall, our review determined that CBT was clearly the most effective treatment out there for binge eating disorder. It leads to decreased frequency of binges, and more people who received CBT reported complete abstinence from binge eating—that means no more binges at all. As delivered in those studies, CBT was not particularly great at reducing weight. This doesn't mean that it can't work, but that the therapies have to be modified to include more direct focus on weight loss and keeping the weight off.

Some other therapies that also showed promise included interpersonal therapy, which focuses on how your relationships in the world are related to your tendency to binge eat, and dialectical behavior therapy, an intensive type of therapy that focuses on learning how to regulate emotions more evenly, and on mindfulness, interpersonal effectiveness, and distress tolerance. We know next to nothing about the treatment of binge eating disorder in children, but if it follows the footsteps of other eating disorders and childhood weight control treatments, then family involvement will be essential.

Some of the specific techniques used in CBT could help you put the principles you are learning in this book to use.

COGNITIVE RESTRUCTURING

If you've ever tried to change a habit or conquer a powerful addiction, you know how incredibly powerful your emotional baggage can be in preventing you from altering something you've been doing for years. Old habits don't only die hard, they also are deeply rooted in our psyches and can make change a real "red alert" situation for the body, mind, and soul whenever you attempt to replace something old (such as your ingrained bingeing behavior) with something new (such as a new form of treatment).

According to cognitive behavioral theory, thoughts and feelings precede actions, and inaccurate thoughts drive unhealthy behaviors. For instance, you feel insecure about standing up in front of your department or class tomorrow and giving a big speech (thoughts and feelings), so you retreat into your safe mode and binge all night (behavior).

What can be done to quell those negative thoughts and feelings that send you into a panic so you don't have so many cues to binge? CBT uses cognitive techniques to challenge such automatic, unhealthy thoughts. For instance, in the above example, when you heard that you had to give a speech your mind immediately—and automatically—imagined the worst about the situation. What if I make an idiot out of myself? What if my mind goes blank? What if I put them to sleep? These negative thoughts became cues for your binge.

But let's look at it another way for a second: Maybe this report you're giving will lead to a promotion at work or higher visibility in your department or a better grade in the class. These are all positive prospects for you to feel good about, not bad. Yes, public speaking can be a huge bugaboo for most of us, but perhaps this is a subject you're really knowledgeable about and have talked about effortlessly in one-on-one situations. Is the fact that you're now doing it in front of ten or twenty people going to stand in the way of all those potential positive outcomes? And maybe it won't be an Academy Award performance, but there are many steps between being an absolute failure and winning an Oscar. It is not an all-or-nothing situation.

That's an example of how CBT focuses on how your negative thoughts can trigger unhealthy behaviors and keep your disordered eating alive. By focusing on the here and now—the reality of the situation as opposed to your unhealthy perception of the situation—CBT can help you redirect the patterns of the past into healthier choices for the future.

For weight control, CBT patients are asked to maintain daily monitoring logs of foods eaten, eating-disordered behaviors, thoughts, feelings, and details about the situation in which these behaviors occurred. This may all sound obsessively structured, but there is freedom in control. The more you know, the more prepared you are when those inevitable cravings return. Healing isn't so much about being cured as it is about being better prepared to deal with urges in a logical, rational, proactive way.

Daily monitoring logs can help you see the patterns that have been occurring before, during, or after your binges. Think about what a great tool that is for the future; knowing that four in the afternoon or midnight are panic-button times for your urges to binge gives you the opportunity to develop strategies ahead of time to deal with them. If you weren't on top of your patterns, you couldn't be prepared.

In addition to learning about food consumed and eating patterns, such self-monitoring reveals patterns of automatic thoughts that reflect broader core beliefs (I am fat. I can't eat this or I am weak. I did well today, I deserve this. I blew it, now I might as well eat more). By identifying such thinking patterns, therapist and patient can better identify and eventually prevent binge eating episodes that might have gone unstopped, or even unnoticed, without therapy.

Over time people become more aware of their automatic thoughts and challenge them; question and evaluate the evidence that supports or invalidates the thoughts; consider alternative views; determine the effect of the automatic thoughts on other thoughts, feelings, and behaviors; and identify typical thinking errors. Finally, given that negative mood and stress can result in overeating, cognitive techniques are used to reduce emotional distress so that individuals refrain from eating during stressful situations.

BEHAVIORAL CHAINING

Behavioral chaining is a visual image that helps us understand how our thoughts, feelings, and behaviors can be linked in long chains of either positive or negative messages. It is also visual in that chains can be broken. Any chain can be broken at any link along the chain, and when you break a link and change a behavior, the rest of the chain changes. Whereas a thought or feeling might result in a binge if you make one choice, it can inspire a walk in the park if you break the chain and make a different choice.

For instance, let's say it's spring and swimsuit season is rapidly upon us. If your first response is "Uh-oh, anxiety alert!" that can be a link in a (negative) behavioral chain. But we know that anxiety can be a trigger in a binge eater, right? Typically, it precedes or even causes a binge. Instead of having a rational response to the first daffodils (hooray, winter's over and summer is almost here), you start to worry and launch a chain of crash or fad diets, overexercising, or worrying. That behavioral chain is just a cascade of self-defeating behaviors, which included several binges along the way.

So what happened? Your behaviors in advance of swimsuit season joined, much like the links of a chain, to create an almost predictable result. First you got anxious about bikini season; then you fretted about not having enough time to get in shape; then you binged because you were fretting constantly, which only made you more anxious. Get the picture?

Like separate links in a chain, your behaviors (overexercising, overeating, bingeing) are linked to your emotions (anxiety, stress, insecurity). The only way to break the chain is to understand it and learn that you have the power to make decisions at every link that could break the chain and drastically affect the outcome.

Behavioral chaining helps you realize that your behavior isn't a runaway train but a series of distinct events, each one of which builds on a former one. You learn the power of removing one link at a time from the chain, and controlling the direction that behavioral chain might ultimately take.

What creates a behavioral chain reaction? Well, it helps to think in terms of cues and consequences. Cues are things that come before and trigger a behavior (like a binge). They can come from inside your head or body (e.g., thoughts, feelings, stomach growling, fatigue, feeling fat, etc.) or from the outside world (e.g., an uncomfortable situation: being lonely, a party, a fight with a loved one, walking past a convenience store, advertisements for food).

Cues lead to consequences (behaviors). In our earlier example, the thought of giving an oral report in front of a group of colleagues or classmates was a cue that led to the consequence of binge eating. Likewise, in our later example, swimsuit season was a cue that resulted in the consequence of several binges that did nothing to reduce the anxiety that triggered them.

Cutting the chain along the way is a powerful approach to learning that you can have control over the choices that you make about your behavior.

RELAPSE PREVENTION

When it comes to successful treatment, relapse is the summer sequel nobody wants to see. Preventing relapse is a central part of any binge eating disorder therapy because it is essential to long-term abstinence from binge eating and successful weight management. The belief is that the endgame of any treatment is independence.

Indeed, treatment programs for binge eating disorder are not designed to go on forever. Instead, the goal of treatment is to foster independence in the patient so that he or she can permanently reap the benefits of treatment. But the secret is that the newfound independence doesn't mean that you forget everything you learned and go back to your old habits and behaviors. You are actually seeking independence from those old patterns as well.

What independence *really* means is that you have taken the tools that you learned in treatment and incorporated them into who you are as a person so that you can draw upon them at will. The same thing is true regarding the skills you learn from this book or from therapy: You now have a toolbox of skills (eat breakfast, identify your triggers, use technology) that you can whip out at a moment's notice if you feel like your behavior is slipping back into old patterns. Not only that, but you also have some insight into what type of professional treatment is available should you start feeling like your own toolbox is just not enough to get you back on track.

Many binge eaters engage in all-or-nothing behavior; I see it all the time. They either have to be perfect or go completely off the rails—and be perfectly miserable as a result. There seems to be no in between for them. Positive aspects of therapy can help them see the difference between having an extra slice of pizza even though they're full and finishing the entire pie just because they had that extra slice. Avoiding all-or-nothing thinking can help prevent a relapse by enabling you to see a particular situation logically as opposed to emotionally; we call this a relapse prevention strategy.

Relapse prevention strategies help individuals identify potential high-risk situations in advance, plan for them (e.g., identify alternative behaviors), and cope by practicing positive thought restructuring (just because I slipped does not mean that I have fallen off the wagon).

Case in point: Going to a party can be a slippery slope for many recovering binge eaters; it can definitely qualify as high risk. But simply identifying the party as high risk arms you against succumbing to it, and here's how.

First, you can prepare. For instance, you know that in the past you might have skipped lunch to "make room" for all of that yummy pizza they'll be serving at the party, but you now know that that strategy will backfire because it sets you up for what basically amounts to a public binge—one, two, three, maybe even four pieces of pizza and an inability to put the brakes on because you are starving. Planning in advance, you have a healthy lunch and a snack before the party so you don't arrive ravenous. You then do a "reconnaissance mission" to see all of the varieties of pizza they have and choose *only* your favorite type. If you feel that your strategies are not going to work to keep you from consuming more, you give yourself permission to walk away, to exit the party to preserve your physical and mental health!

Another relapse prevention strategy is what we call a "panic card." A panic card (including positive self-statements, alternative behaviors, and even social support phone numbers) can help you when you come face-to-face with a high-risk situation before your mind fuzzes over and you forget the skills that you have learned.

For instance, let's say your experience with the pizza party from above didn't go as well as planned. An old boyfriend showed up who has a curious habit of pressing your buttons (and one of those buttons is the "on" switch for binge eating). You were not able to resist pizza slices two and three, and you couldn't muster up the energy to walk away. At that stage you can't rely on your brain to get you out of the situation on your own. You need help, and there's no better help than your own thoughts and actions developed at a time when you were feeling more in control.

That's where the panic card comes in. During a rational and strong period, you constructed your panic card (a basic three-by-five-inch index card custom-designed for times like this) and stuck copies in your wallet, purse, glove compartment, backpack, or all of the above. When you do not have the strength or presence of mind to think clearly and behave rationally, the panic card lays out a step-by-step plan for you to follow. With it in hand, all you have to do is read and obey to get through the high-risk period.

What could you put on the card? That's up to you, but here are some suggestions:

1. Phone numbers of people you can rely on to call for help in getting you over the hump or distracting you from the situation.

2. Affirming statements such as "I've gotten out of these situations before; I can do it again" or "There's no shame in avoiding a situation that is too high risk" or "You have the skills to manage this, but it is just tough to use them now—give yourself a break."

3. "Orders" to leave the party (or whatever the situation) and:

   • Go for a drive without taking any money.
   • Listen to a particularly affirming or calming playlist on your iPod.
   • Take a shower and wash your hair.

All of these suggestions get you out of the high-risk situation. When panic strikes there is no shame in using the panic card. It can help!

Medication

You can pop a pill for your blood pressure and for your cholesterol, but you can't just pop a pill for binge eating disorder. There is no medication specifically approved by the FDA to treat binge eating disorder, and definitely no medication that can eliminate urges to binge.

That being said, there are several medications that may be helpful in your recovery if this is a direction you are comfortable taking. Some examples include the group of antidepressants known as selective serotonin reuptake inhibitors (SSRIs), certain appetite suppressants, and specific antiseizure medications such as topiramate (Topamax) that can also help reduce your urges to binge.

The important thing to remember about medication and binge eating disorder is that we have found no magic pill that addresses the myriad components that go into recovery from binge eating disorder, in essence because it is simply too complicated biologically and psychologically to be relieved by a cure-all capsule. What we found instead was that medication could help and did best when combined with a psychological intervention.

The biggest problem is that there is no evidence that you could or should stay on these medications for the rest of your life, and when you stop taking them, if you haven't developed any other skills to curb your cravings and binges, those behaviors might just come right back. Medication was more effective than cognitive behavioral therapy in targeting the weight loss component of binge eating disorder treatment, however.

For that reason, the combination of CBT plus medication may be an effective way to target both binge eating and weight loss. Unfortunately, we don't yet have the optimal combination to lead to long-lasting behavioral change and weight-loss maintenance. But all that means is that you may need to explore until you find the combination that works for you. The best place to start is talking with your physician about suitable medications.

Behavioral Weight-loss Programs

More so than psychotherapy, weight-loss programs focus on losing excess body weight. They're typically conducted under medical supervision to ensure that nutritional requirements are met. Some programs are known as very low calorie diet programs because they include an initial period of extreme calorie restriction for fast results.

Weight-loss programs may also address issues that tend to trigger binges, but often to a lesser extent than psychotherapy does. However, weight-loss programs, especially those that are not medically supervised, may not be appropriate for everyone with binge eating disorder. These programs typically aren't recommended until the binge eating disorder is treated. In some cases, very low calorie diets can trigger more binge-eating episodes, which only serve to make the condition worse.

The behavioral approach for weight control or obesity includes many of the core techniques (sometimes with different names) that we have introduced here. Some of these include dietary recommendations, exercise, cognitive techniques, stimulus control, relapse prevention, and social support. Although weight loss is certainly the goal of treatment, the focus is on behavior change.

The treatment requires a patient's active participation; it is goal oriented, problem focused, and structured, while using many techniques to change distorted thinking, mood, and thus problematic behavior. If you find that participation in such a program helps you with weight control and does not trigger binges, then it may be an option worth keeping in your toolbox.

Nutrition Education

It is important for everyone to understand the difference between healthy eating and unhealthy eating. Emotional eating (eating for any reason other than physiological necessity—i.e., out of boredom, anger, frustration, excitement, etc.), eating in response to cravings or urges (which is also often linked to emotional reasons), and unhealthy dieting (purging, restricting, or viewing a diet as something of limited duration rather than a healthy permanent lifestyle change) are examples of unhealthy eating, which may result in both physical problems (intense hunger, low energy, fatigue, headaches, visual problems, weight gain, electrolyte disturbance, dental problems, gastrointestinal problems), cognitive problems (focus on food, loss of interest, poor concentration, memory problems, difficulty with comprehension and decision making), and emotional problems (stress, irritability, anxiety, and depression).

Visiting a dietician is a great idea. She or he can help you develop healthier eating habits. A dietician can also help with selecting and preparing meals, establishing guidelines for how much to eat and portion control, and patterning your eating (number of meals and snacks per day) to fit your needs and your lifestyle. One of the things that I have found is that dieticians can help us get out of eating ruts. Sometimes our approaches to family meals—what we cook and how we cook it—get passed down through the generations without much thought.

It becomes one of those "that's how we've always done it" sort of ordeals. Dieticians can show you how to shake things up and introduce new and effective ways of planning and preparing meals, such as using ingredients that aren't currently part of your cooking vocabulary. After a visit with a dietician, you might experience the grocery store in a completely new way—seeing ingredients on the shelves that you might never even have looked at before.

Self-help Approaches

Some people with binge eating disorder find self-help books, videos, and support groups effective. Some eating-disorder programs even offer self-help manuals that you can use on your own or with guidance from mental health experts. In the United Kingdom, self-help is not only seen as a positive step toward recovery from binge eating disorder, but is also actually recommended as the first step in treating it.

In our government report, the science revealed that self-help approaches were effective in decreasing binge eating. So following the advice in this book and in other self-help aids can and will work if you stick with it.

Twelve-Step Programs

Did you know that Botox was originally used to treat people with blepharospasm, or involuntary squinting of the eyes? Or that it was explored for potential military use in biological warfare? Over the years, it was also used to treat spasmodic dysphonia, a severe condition of the vocal cords, as well as the separate condition of overly sweaty armpits or palms. Eventually, however, plastic surgeons realized that what helped restore normal speaking voices and reduce eye spasms could also erase wrinkles from foreheads and around the eyes. Turns out, what worked for one problem could also work for another.

By the same token, what if you could conquer binge eating disorder with the twelve steps that have already been proven to conquer another addiction? Most people know about Alcoholics Anonymous (AA) and that it employs a twelve-step approach based on the need for abstinence from alcohol. The AA approach begins with the realization that the individual is powerless over the addiction, and provides a structured step-by-step approach to remaining sober.

There are regular meetings worldwide and a sponsor who can be called if a member is feeling unable to maintain sobriety or is in need of support. Participants are acknowledged for each year of sobriety and social support is a central component of the intervention.

Well, alcohol isn't the only problem for which a twelve-step approach exists. Many people with binge eating disorder who have tried everything else report that Overeaters Anonymous (OA) provides them with the guidance and structure they need in order to control their binge eating.

THE OA PROGRAM OF RECOVERY

Overeaters Anonymous offers a program of recovery from compulsive overeating using the Twelve Steps and Twelve Traditions of OA. Worldwide meetings and other tools provide a fellowship of experience, strength, and hope where members respect one another's anonymity. OA charges no dues or fees; it is self-supporting through member contributions.

Unlike other organizations, OA is not just about weight loss, obesity, or diets; it addresses physical, emotional, and spiritual well-being. It is not a religious organization and does not promote any particular diet. To address weight loss, OA encourages members to develop a food plan with a health care professional and a sponsor.[4]

Some people swear by Overeaters Anonymous, but because OA asks its members to acknowledge that they are powerless over food it has been controversial in the therapeutic community, which typically aims to help patients feel they are in control of their behavior. Anecdotally, I have dealt with people who found that the moderation path just does not work for them and find that they benefit from an Overeaters Anonymous approach. I have not found any similarities that unite these people—except that OA was the last thing they tried and it helped them control their otherwise uncontrollable eating.

Resources

Knowledge is power. Many people with binge eating disorder find that getting accurate, up-to-date information about their condition empowers them to take the steps they need to take to get well. There are some terrible resources out there, but here we point you toward the excellent ones. This little reference section lists the organizations and other sources where you can find immediate, reliable, and trustworthy help.

Many of these organizations also have annual meetings, family and friends organizations, Listservs, referral services, and advocacy groups. You should feel free to seek out information as well as support from other individuals in your position who are also looking for information and support.

ACADEMY FOR EATING DISORDERS

Located in Deerfield, Illinois, the Academy for Eating Disorders (AED) strives for both education and practicality as it grows along with the number of eating disorder cases it sees every year. Advocacy and understanding are the foundations of this well-respected academy.

The mission statement is from their Web site. "The Academy for Eating Disorders (AED) is a global, multidisciplinary professional organization that provides cutting-edge professional training and education, inspires new developments in eating disorders research, prevention, and clinical treatments, and is the international source for state-of-the-art information in the field of eating disorders."

CONTACT INFORMATION
Academy for Eating Disorders
AED Headquarters
111 Deer Lake Road, Suite 100
Deerfield, IL 60015
Telephone: (847) 498-4274
Fax: (847) 480-9282
E-mail: info@aedweb.org
Web site: www.aedweb.org

Eating Disorders Coalition

The Eating Disorders Coalition's mission is "to advance the federal recognition of eating disorders as a public health priority . . . With more focused attention on educating and working with Congress we can effectively influence federal policy." This is the group that lobbies on Capitol Hill in order to improve funding for research on, treatment of, and education about eating disor-

---

Tips for Talking to a Friend Who May Be Struggling with a Binge Eating Disorder

If you are worried about your friend or loved one's eating behaviors or attitudes, it is important to express your concerns in a loving and supportive way. It is also necessary to discuss your worries early on, rather than waiting until your friend has endured many of the damaging physical and emotional effects of eating disorders.

Set aside a time for a private, respectful meeting with your friend to discuss your concerns openly and honestly in a caring, supportive way. Make sure you will be someplace free from distractions.

Communicate your concerns. Share your memories of specific times when you felt concerned about your friend's eating or exercise behaviors. Explain that you think these things may indicate that there could be a problem that needs professional attention.

Ask your friend to explore these concerns with a counselor, doctor, nutritionist, or other health care professional who is knowledgeable about eating issues. If you feel comfortable doing so, offer to help your friend make an appointment or accompany your friend on his or her first visit.

If your friend refuses to acknowledge that there is a problem or that there is any reason for you to be concerned, restate your

ders. They also work toward improving insurance coverage and getting eating disorders recognized as serious illnesses worthy of adequate insurance coverage.

CONTACT INFORMATION
Eating Disorders Coalition
720 7th St. NW, Suite 300
Washington, DC, 20001-3902

feelings and the reasons for them and leave yourself open and available as a supportive listener. Avoid conflicts or a battle of wills.

Avoid placing shame, blame, or guilt on your friend regarding his or her actions or attitudes. Do not use accusatory "you" statements like "You went to three separate drive-through restaurants for lunch yesterday." Or "You left a wad of junk food wrappers under the driver's seat again yesterday." Instead, use "I" statements. For example: "I am concerned about you because you've been avoiding eating with me more than usual lately." Or "It makes me afraid to see food disappearing from the fridge when you say you've got your binge eating disorder beat."

Avoid giving simple solutions. For example, "If you'd just stop, then everything would be fine!"

Express your continued support. Remind your friend that you care and want him or her to be healthy and happy.

After talking with your friend, if you are still concerned with his or her health and safety, find a trusted medical professional with whom to talk. This is probably a challenging time for both of you. It could be helpful for you, as well as your friend, to discuss your concerns and seek assistance and support from a professional.[5]

Telephone: (202) 543-9570
Web site: www.eatingdisorderscoalition.org

NATIONAL EATING DISORDERS ASSOCIATION

If you're looking for specialists in eating disorders, the National Eating Disorders Association (NEDA) can help. Formed in 2001, NEDA has worked toward preventing eating disorders, providing access to quality treatment, and increasing funding for research to better understand and treat eating disorders. NEDA's mission statement is as follows: "NEDA supports individuals and families affected by eating disorders and serves as a catalyst for prevention, cures, and access to quality care."

CONTACT INFORMATION
National Eating Disorders Association (NEDA)
603 Stewart St., Suite 803
Seattle, WA 98101
Telephone: (206) 382-3587
Toll-free Information and Referral Helpline: (800) 931-2237
E-mail: info@NationalEatingDisorders.org
Web site: www.nationaleatingdisorders.org

NATIONAL INSTITUTE OF MENTAL HEALTH

Long recognized as a go-to source for all things mental health related, the National Institute of Mental Health (NIMH) offers a wide variety of information and services for those in need. According to their Web site, "The National Institute of Mental Health (NIMH) provides information to help people better understand mental health, mental disorders, and behavioral problems. NIMH does not provide referrals to mental health professionals or treatment for mental health problems."

CONTACT INFORMATION
6001 Executive Boulevard
Room 8184, MSC 9663
Bethesda, MD 20892-9663
Telephone: (301) 443-4513
Toll-free: (866) 615-6464
Fax: (301) 443-4279
E-mail: nimhinfo@nih.gov
Web site: www.nimh.nih.gov

BINGE EATING DISORDER ASSOCIATION

The Binge Eating Disorder Association (BEDA) is an international multidisciplinary provider and patient organization. The mission of BEDA is to focus on unmet needs for preventing, diagnosing, and treating binge eating disorder. BEDA is committed to facilitating awareness, quality of care, and recovery for those who live and those who work with binge eating disorder through education, resources, research, and best-practice guidelines.

CONTACT INFORMATION
637 Emerson Place
Severna Park, MD 21146
Telephone: (410) 570-9577
Fax: (410) 741-3037
E-mail: info@bedaonline.com
Web site: www.bedaonline.com

PART III

Beyond the Binge

During treatment you will hit resistance, plateaus, and barriers along the road to recovery. It's only natural to encounter obstacles as you try to change years—maybe even decades—of old eating habits. The tools in this section will help you handle those roadblocks with passion and precision.

CHAPTER 10

"You Call *This* Fat?"

You have to have curves ... You can't look like a stick-thin model.
—KIRSTEN HAGLUND, MISS AMERICA 2008

Many know actor Dennis Quaid as the underdog pitcher in *The Rookie*. Others may recognize him as a befuddled president from *American Dreamz*, the fading football star in *Any Given Sunday*, or even famed wild man Jerry Lee Lewis in the bio-pic *Great Balls of Fire*. If you're a parent, you've probably seen him as the harried father of eighteen children in the family classic *Yours, Mine, and Ours*.

But few who watched him glower on the screen as Doc Holliday in *Wyatt Earp* knew that he had an an eating disorder. Quaid coined a trendy term, "manorexic," while speaking for the first time about his own battles with the disease.

He reportedly lost forty pounds to play the emaciated Wild West gunslinger in the western epic *Wyatt Earp*, and the sudden weight loss began a decade-long quest—through most of the

1990s—to maintain that weight. Quoted in *Best Life* magazine recently, Quaid explained, "My arms were so skinny that I couldn't pull myself out of a pool . . . I wasn't bulimic, but I could understand what people go through with that . . . I'd look in the mirror and still see a 180-pound guy, even though I was 138 pounds."[1]

He is far from unique. Quaid's story—along with those of countless actresses including Paula Abdul, Justine Bateman, Tracey Gold, and Jamie-Lynn Sigler—reflects a deeper problem that extends beyond the Hollywood community and sends ripples throughout the rest of the country.

In short, we are a country with a crisis—an identity crisis. We are so often bombarded with images of perfection as the ultimate aesthetic goal that we naturally tend to focus on our inadequacies as opposed to our strengths and uniqueness. Today you can buy almost any body you want. Before the age of plastic surgery, stomach stapling, liposuction, extreme dieting, supplements, and the fitness craze, we were all stuck with the body the good Lord gave us.

Today we've reached the age where technology and medicine make it possible to literally transcend our genes. We've become "modifiable humans." We are no longer bound by our height, our features, our shape, our eye color, or our weight. Those of us who can afford it can create "designer bodies." Society, the media, popular culture, and our peers pressure us toward vanity-based changes.

But what about when we are pushed, either directly or indirectly, by professions that demand alterations in our natural selves in order to get the job? From jockeys who are forced to become unnaturally thin to football players who are told to beef up, to porn stars with penile and quadruple D breast implants, to models who starve to achieve the "heroin-chic" ideal, all of these unwritten expectations have the same message: Change your body or find another job.

Of course, we don't have to be in the public eye or professional sports to feel these pressures. What about the over-weight waitress who applies at a Hooters? The pale, gangly nerd who wants to dance at Chippendales? And who hasn't gone in to apply for a job and, seeing the natural beauty of the recep-tionist or the vibrant youthfulness of the other employees—not to mention the other applicants—felt that physical attractive-ness was literally a prerequisite for the new job?

Our appearance can cost more than self-esteem; it can cost cold, hard cash. Writing on behalf of *The Regional Economist*, a publication of the Federal Reserve Bank of St. Louis, authors Kristie M. Engemann and Michael T. Owyang report, "a person with below-average looks tended to earn 9 percent less per hour, and an above-average person tended to earn 5 percent more per hour than an average-looking person."[2]

The promise of body-altering procedures and schemes is al-ways the same: A more perfect body will lead to a happier life. Forget personality, intelligence, talent, creativity, humor, wit, street smarts, or plain old common sense; "look good first" seems to be the overriding message we get these days. Only the packaging counts.

What physical and psychological dangers lurk behind these extreme alterations? What are the long-term effects on health and quality of life? What are the permanent scars? What hap-pens when you are past your use-by date?

We live in a world of increasing extremes that includes more anorexia on one end and more binge eating on the other. Many of the same outrageous environmental forces can actu-ally influence the development of both conditions.

Signs of hope that the awareness level is changing are be-ginning to become evident. Dove cosmetics recently made bestselling author and self-esteem expert Jessica Weiner their "global ambassador" in a new strategy called Campaign for Real Beauty, "a global effort designed to widen today's stereo-typical view of beauty." Says Weiner, "Impossible standards of beauty are not confined to Hollywood, they pervade every

aspect of girls' lives no matter where they live, often with
alarming consequences like eating disorders and self-inflicted
injury."[3]

Model Tyra Banks, tennis star Serena Williams, plus-size
model Emme, and actress Jennifer Love Hewitt are among the
celebrities who have fought back about being molded by our
media-dominated culture by speaking out against the American obsession with weight.

How did they do it? How did they buck the trends and find
their own definition of inner and outer beauty? In this chapter
I'll present the strategies they used. You can transform them
into workable solutions to help you cope with the unhelpful
attitudes of family members, bosses, and friends.

A ROSE BY ANY OTHER NAME—FROM "AHOLICS" TO "OREXIAS"

Not so long ago everybody seemed to be an "aholic." We had
shopaholics, sexaholics, and chocaholics. We seem to have
moved seamlessly out of the "aholic" phase and into the
"orexia" phase with some "imias" thrown in.

So far I have seen "stressorexia" (obsessed with stress), "drunkorexia" (alcoholism and anorexia nervosa), "orthorexia" (eats only
health foods to feel pure or natural), "tanorexia" (obsessed with
getting a tan), "whiteorexia" (obsessed with teeth whitening),
"manorexia" (anorexia nervosa in a man), "wannarexia" (someone who wishes they could be anorexic to lose weight), "prego-
rexia" (undereating during pregnancy), and "diabulimia"
(diabetes and bulimia).

The Academy for Eating Disorders has concerns about these
terms. They worry that turning everything into an "orexia" or an
"imia" desensitizes the public to or trivializes the seriousness of
true eating disorders such as anorexia nervosa, bulimia nervosa, and binge eating disorder, when in fact we know eating

Bariatric Surgery and Binge Eating Disorder

Many people consider bariatric surgery to be the gold standard for body modification. Much has been made of the surgery, from celebrities profiled on TV or in *People* magazine to hundreds of Web sites touting the benefits of the procedure. There are even "bariatric diet kits" to help control weight gain after the surgery.

Now, let me say from the outset that I am in no way opposed to bariatric surgery. There are definitely people who have tried every alternative and whose health is in clear danger without the procedure. I have seen lives transformed, and what has been fascinating to me is how motivating the surgery can be for changing your lifestyle! But that being said, I don't think

---

disorders are serious illnesses with severe consequences for both physical and psychological health.

What some of these labels are describing is comorbidity, something that is even more severe than a single eating disorder. We talked about the comorbidity of binge eating disorder and anxiety and depression, but "drunkorexia" is a specious label for someone who might be suffering from the deadly combination of alcoholism and anorexia nervosa. Likewise, the potentially lethal combination of diabetes and bulimia tagged as "diabulimia" misses the fact that the risk of diabetic complications skyrockets in individuals with bulimia—especially when they manipulate their insulin for weight-loss purposes.

Other "orexia" labels really *are* just describing the obsessive behavior—with tanning, tooth whitening, or whatever. But don't be fooled. Although none of these labels is a real diagnosis, they can signify double trouble and must be taken seriously.

that everyone with a weight problem should go out and think about surgery as a quick fix. In other words, it can be an effective alternative for those who have exhausted other healthy means of weight loss through diet and exercise, but I caution against the trend of skipping the alternatives and going straight to the surgery.

Although there are several types of bariatric surgery, including the popular Lap-Band procedure, most such surgeries involve the Roux-en-Y gastric bypass, in which the stomach is actually made smaller. Since the stomach can now hold less food, people eat less after such surgeries and, as a result, often lose a significant amount of weight.

Who can qualify for bariatric surgery and what is the impact of binge eating disorder on the outcome?

Weight-loss surgery programs, such as that at the University of North Carolina at Chapel Hill, follow guidelines for patient candidacy established during a 1991 NIH consensus conference on gastrointestinal surgery for severe obesity. These state that adults are candidates for surgery if they are morbidly obese (with a BMI greater than $40\,kg/m^2$ or greater than or equal to $35\,kg/m^2$ with comorbidities), have failed in their attempts at diet and exercise, are motivated and well informed, and are free of significant psychological disease. Surgeon Timothy M. Farrell, M.D., from the University of North Carolina at Chapel Hill is quick to add that "for an individual patient, the expected benefits of the operation must outweigh the risks." While it is true that surgery for morbid obesity is effective for most patients, with an average loss of 61.2 percent of excess weight, the risks of surgery may reach 20 percent, depending on the operation chosen.

Dr. Farrell points out that patients considering weight-loss surgery are more likely than the overall population to have binge eating disorder, and that poor control of their binge eating may result in a suboptimal outcome after the operation. He underscores that while there are no agreed-upon recommendations in terms of preoperative psychological evaluation, nearly all U.S. weight-loss surgery programs employ some psychological evaluation, with half requiring a formal standardized assessment. Unfortunately, from what I have seen elsewhere, the procedure is ripe for negligence. Sometimes the initial psychological evaluation is perfunctory on the clinic's behalf; other times people are so desperate for the procedure that they lie or don't fully disclose during the psychiatric evaluation. In some cases, the consult never quite happens at all.

According to Dr. Farrrell, careful screening and follow-up by a nutritionist is an integral part of pre- and postoperative care, with specific focus on identification of eating disorders to tailor postoperative education in order to achieve the best outcomes. Nevertheless, the bulk of evidence shows no relationship between pre-existing psychiatric diagnoses (including binge eating disorder) and total weight loss from bariatric surgery.

"These procedures provide most patients with dramatic weight loss and a second chance to reconfigure their lives," emphasizes Dr. Farrell. "Those who are passive in adjusting behaviors and utilizing support services after the surgery may fail over time. Those who see their operation as part of a bigger life change, who are willing to make time to exercise regularly and attend support groups, who work with professionals to keep control of other medical and psychological conditions, and who follow through with the maintenance protocols prescribed by the surgeon will reap the benefits. Weight-loss surgery is the first step on a long journey."[4]

It is understandable that this would seem like a lifesaver for some individuals. Think about it; if you're one hundred pounds overweight (or more, as is often the case) and have been battling weight and self-esteem issues for years, the desperation to do something about it could easily lead you to tell the doctor what he or she wants to hear—almost anything—in order to be cleared for surgery.

The fact of the matter is that requirements for the surgery

are so loosely defined that if you want it, chances are, you can get it. But then what? What does the research say about how bariatric surgery—Lap-Band or gastric bypass—affects binge eating disorder? Well, as is often the case when new procedures become very popular very quickly, the jury is still out. Some studies suggest that bariatric surgery actually decreases binge eating. Others say that people just change how they eat. Don't think that just because your stomach is smaller you can't binge eat; you can, only in smaller quantities. The physical satiety may be more easily reached, but the desire, the craving, may still be there, strong as ever, unless you train your mind to guard against such cravings by following the principles in this book.

It is also important to separate the physical from the mental when it comes to your disorder. Recognize that bariatric surgery is only a physical solution to a physical problem; if you are at least one hundred pounds overweight and traditional weight-loss methods have failed, chances are bariatric surgery will allow you to lose that excess weight. Physically speaking, at least, you can reasonably expect to achieve that very specific goal.

In fact, studies have shown that binge eating does not put you at greater risk for complications and/or weight loss after your bariatric surgery. Speaking to Reuters Health, Dr. Marney A. White from Yale University School of Medicine explained, "Overall, preoperative binge eating does not appear to be a negative prognostic indicator for surgery in the initial twelve-month period following surgery, in that patients—regardless of binge eating status—show dramatic improvements in terms of weight loss and psychosocial functioning."[5]

No physical surgery can excise the genetic factors or triggers that led to your binge eating disorder, so to link them inextricably is only dooming yourself to failure. Recognize that despite the weight loss, you may very well still have urges to binge, and guard against them by using the tools provided in this book together with engaging in a healthy lifestyle that nourishes both the body and the mind.

Going Too Far to Stay in the Game

The world of both amateur and professional sports is no stranger to the subject of body modification. In fact, if anything, the sports world has for the most part flown under the radar for the past few decades when it comes to creating "modifiable humans." Recent reports have come to light, however, that uncover a strange and hybrid world where body modification includes the use of steroids or growth hormones to improve performance, often with disastrous, and even deadly, consequences.

The recent rash of steroid use is yet another indicator that our national identity crisis is manifesting itself in dangerous extremes. The reason people take steroids in the first place is to modify their bodies and to increase appearance or performance by artificial means. But are football players bulking up to play on the defensive line any different from high school wrestlers starving themselves to make the next lowest weight division? In both cases, the way they *are* is no longer enough to do the job they are being asked to do. The expectations of their sport literally require them to bulk up or slim down—to change themselves physically. Many athletes engage in unhealthy and unwise eating in order to do this.

The discovery that binge eating can be triggered by prolonged periods of extreme dieting has dire consequences for professional jockeys—so dire that the National Institute of Occupational Health and Safety (NIOSH) initiated public hearings in 2007 on health concerns in the horse racing industry.[6]

I was invited to attend, both to assist with providing background on eating-disorders issues and to help explore how the proceedings regarding jockeys might be relevant to other industries that force people to change their body shape or size in order to get a job.

Like boxers, jockeys are athletes who are required to weigh in before they participate in a sanctioned event in their sport. Like actors, they must "audition" for each race, auditioning that includes weight-based decisions. As a result they regularly "pull weight" (stop eating, take diuretics, gobble weight-loss pills, or purge—"flipping" in jockey terms—and sweat off water weight in a "hot box") on a regular basis to stay below the limit.

But how long can their bodies endure this deprivation and abuse? Since many start riding as young boys, they never learn proper eating habits. After retirement and no longer having to go on extreme diets, jockeys who might be genetically vulnerable to binge eating quickly pack on extra pounds and go on eating binges they feel powerless to stop. Many develop rampant type 2 diabetes as a result.

I am reminded of the touching scene in *Seabiscuit* where the young jockey played by Tobey Maguire, thinking his career is over in the wake of Seabiscuit's injuries, gorges himself at dinner; he is literally free of the bonds of deprivation and reacts accordingly.

What lengths will jockeys go to in order to stay competitive in the sport? One survey showed that of those interviewed:

- 60 percent reported weekly use of laxatives, diuretics (usually prescribed Lasix), diet pills, and other meds
- 32 percent had a chronically low BMI (body mass index, the accepted measurement of body fatness or thinness)
- 80 percent use the "hot box," with 25 percent using it daily

Among the damning statistics I learned in connection with this sport is that exercise riders, those who train and warm up horses for stables, regularly weigh between 140 and 150 pounds, whereas jockeys, together with their equipment, weigh around 120 pounds. Yet there are no ill effects of having heavier riders on the thoroughbreds, according to testimony from Dr. David Seftel, medical adviser to the Jockeys Guild. Moreover, U.S. weight standards are below Australia, Ireland, the United Kingdom, New Zealand, and other countries where horse racing is a popular sport.

The weight issue forces some jockeys to exist in a constant state of deprivation. Jockey quarters often favor emaciation, as they come equipped with a "hot box" for sweating off pounds and specially shaped toilets for purging. Jockeys' immune systems become compromised due to low weight and poor nutrition, and their performance suffers because of low blood sugar, lack of coordination, and dizziness.

Dr. Seftel contends that low weight standards currently in effect in states with professional horse-racing tracks result in "state-mandated malnutrition." Although more data are needed, the industry should consider making nutrition competency a mandatory part of getting one's jockey qualification. Meanwhile, the NIOSH investigation has trained a spotlight on this neglected quarter of professional athletes' health.

Glamorizing Size Zero

Looking through my closet the other day, I was reminded of an old *M*A*S*H* episode. In this very memorable installment, Hawkeye and Hunnicutt (Alan Alda and Mike Farrell, respectively) decide to play yet another practical joke on their brilliant but gullible roommate, Major Charles Emerson Winchester III, played by David Ogden Stiers. Since Major Winchester is a husky guy with a fondness for food, they decide to play fast and loose with his pants size, figuring to take the famously egotistical Winchester down a notch or two in the process.

One day he goes to get into his fatigues and they're too tight; so he restricts a little food in the mess hall and, the next day, his pants are two sizes too big! Thinking he's found a miracle diet he keeps restricting, but the pants get tighter and tighter; he restricts some more and suddenly the pants are far too loose. Hawkeye and Hunnicutt's prank teaches Major Winchester that you can't always trust what's on the label.

What does a practical joke on a hit TV show have to do with my own closet? Two words: *vanity sizing*. Perhaps in your closet you have skirts and slacks that are actually the same size; yet one is labeled 18, one 16, one 14, and another 10. Manufacturers of women's clothing have responded to our epidemic weight gain by downsizing. They are labeling clothes to seem smaller not larger so that you think you're not fat. This simple mind game makes us feel better because we think we're wearing a smaller size. At the same time, though, it's telling us that only a size 0 will do.

What does it mean to be a size 0? In my mind, it means not to exist. Zero is an anti-number; it means nothing. And yet dressmakers, fashion designers, and retail stores now hold up the mythical size 0 as the ultimate desirable size.

What is the metamessage that we are giving young girls? That we shouldn't take up space? That to be attractive and glamorous you have to not exist? And what is a size 00? Less than nothing. What if you're too tiny for a 0? Does that make you a negative number—an inverse person? It is all patently absurd, and yet in our brave new world of modifiable humans, it's all the rage.

Recently, a rash of beautiful young actresses have had to come to their own defense against the crushing paparazzi trend of snapping unflattering photos of their most intimate moments. Most famously, when *Ghost Whisperer* actress Jennifer Love Hewitt was widely tweaked for showing a little cellulite while frolicking on the beach in her bikini, she had to publicly declare, "A size 2 is *not* fat!"

Katie Couric found herself in a miniscandal when airbrushed promotional photos surfaced showing her looking much slimmer than she really was in the original photo, and an image of Faith Hill on the cover of a popular women's magazine was shown to have been manipulated in Photoshop. While the trend of manipulating images is certainly nothing new (*Playboy* and many fashion magazines have been "airbrushing" models for years), the trend is yet another instance of our becoming modifiable humans. In other words, if we can't be physically perfect, at least our images can.

Another disturbing trend is the more recent "yummy mummy" craze, in which women no longer feel it's acceptable to gradually, and one might argue safely, lose their "baby bump" in the months after giving birth. Now the trend is not only to work out before pregnancy but as long as possible during and afterward.

Dancing with the Stars cohost Samantha Harris returned to network television to pick up her hosting duties a mere three weeks after giving birth! She'd already been working out for nearly a week by that point, and many were amazed by how quickly she was back in top form. She isn't alone. Many were amazed by how quickly Nicole Richie shed her baby weight; and Heidi Klum was back on the catwalk a mere seven weeks after giving birth to her son Henry. Fashion magazines routinely comment not only on how these new moms "glow" but also about how thin they are. The message is undeniable: Only "yummie mummies" deserve respect and admiration.

The problem with most of these trends is perception: From our comfy living rooms and beauty parlor chairs, we see various Hollywood moms bouncing back to their prepregnancy forms in world-record time. "Why can't we do that?" we ask ourselves. But what we're forgetting is that Hollywood moms are not the norm; many of them have personal trainers and nannies as well as chefs who prepare healthy low-calorie meals. Having full-time help and flexible schedules gives them plenty of time to exercise. Most people can't afford this luxury.

After Kate Hudson had her son, Ryder, she reportedly hired

two personal trainers and worked out from two to three hours per day, six days a week, to get back in shape. You and I don't have time for that, nor would we even *want* to put that much time into working out. But for a woman like Ms. Hudson, at the peak of her earning potential eager to get back to making a seven- or eight-figure salary for her next film, there's a greater incentive.

Obviously, it is a highly paid Hollywood mom's job to get back in fighting shape weeks after birth. Samantha Harris had a top-rated show to cohost; that was her job. These women can hire others to help with mundane tasks, allowing them to focus on their jobs and their babies. If you don't have a lifestyle that enables you to hire plenty of extra help, then give yourself time to get some sleep, get your strength back, and nurture your baby.

Post-pregnancy crash dieting leads to fatigue and does not allow you to sustain breastfeeding, which confers so many health benefits on your baby (and you!), possibly even a healthier body weight throughout life! Women get so many compliments for getting back to their prepregnancy weight quickly when that really should not be their focus; they need to be allowed to be mothers—to be allowed recovery time and bonding time without worrying about whether or not they can get back into a size 0.

Bingeing with Baby

Binge eating disorder does not go on holiday just because you're pregnant. In fact when you're pregnant, simple cravings and extra snacks are par for the course; a pickle here, a peanut butter and mayonnaise taco there.

It's when your eating gets out of control—when cravings turn to binges—that you need to worry. Studying over forty thousand pregnant women in Norway, my colleagues from the Norwegian Institute of Public Health and my team found that many women who had never had an eating disorder developed one—in this case, binge eating disorder—during pregnancy.[7]

For many years, physicians assumed that women who had eating disorders went into some degree of "remission" during their pregnancy. However, my colleagues and I discovered that although this happened for many women, for others just the opposite was true: that women who already had binge eating disorder were more likely to continue bingeing than they were to go into remission.

What should you be on the lookout for if you find yourself battling excessive—or excessively strong—cravings during pregnancy? Many women often find that they do get incredibly hungry during pregnancy. I remember telling my husband that I didn't just feel hungry; that my very bones felt hungry. This also happened when I was breastfeeding. My body was giving me a clear message: Feed the baby! But in my case it was truly hunger—not an urge to binge and not a craving. And, I did not have that telltale sign of feeling out of control.

If you are having strong urges to binge during pregnancy and you feel like your eating is spinning out of control, don't wait; get yourself to a dietician and health-care provider immediately. We do not yet appreciate the impact of binge eating during pregnancy on either the birth outcomes or on the baby's health and development. But now that we recognize that this *is* a problem, it is better to be safe than sorry and to get your erratic eating under control before you find out that there may be negative consequences to you or the baby.

Measuring with a New Yardstick:
Tips, Tactics and Strategies for Finding Your Own Self-Worth

In summary, if you were to believe everything you read, saw, and heard coming out of Hollywood and New York, you would

A NEW TWIST ON AN OLD PAGEANT

If we're talking about societal pressures on American women to have unrealistic expectations of their modifiable bodies, I would be remiss in not mentioning the venerable Miss America pageant. For years beauty pageants have helped foster an image of Vaselined-toothed, sprayed-on smiles, and sucked-in tummies.

Feminists and social researchers alike have long contended that pageants are sexist and demeaning to women. Yet new signs emerge that the pageants could be changing—for the better.

Recently, Miss America 2008, Kirsten Haglund, announced that she "plans to spend her year-long reign trying to raise awareness of eating disorders." Turns out Kirsten, like many pageant participants, has struggled with eating, culminating only three years ago with a diagnosis of anorexia nervosa.

"I would feel fatigued walking up six stairs," explained the nineteen-year-old Haglund to the press after being crowned Miss America 2008. "I was a completely different person. It's not a pretty sight."[8]

I had the honor of speaking with Miss Haglund at a congressional briefing on Capitol Hill in April 2007 conducted by the Eating Disorders Coalition and sponsored by Congressman Patrick Kennedy (D-RI). I was deeply impressed with her maturity and positivity during her efforts to spread awareness of eating disorders while in the national spotlight.

Many participants have been afraid to admit they had an eating disorder, fearing repercussions or having it count against them in pageants. Her courage in telling her story has helped bring eating disorders out of the shadows in the pageant world, and there is no question that her honesty will help scores of young women feel more comfortable seeking help with their struggles. When asked to reveal her weight, for instance, the newest Miss America steadfastly refuses, "to avoid setting standards for youths obsessed with being lighter."

be convinced that everyone is the "perfect" version of the human form: blemish-fee, o percent body fat, silky, shiny hair—all in the right places.

But we all know those are goals that for the average person are impossible to achieve (let alone maintain), particularly without the aid of personal trainers and chefs, not to mention the time it takes to focus all your energy on your physical form. Still, the notion persists that if we can just look a certain way, get to a certain weight, reach the perfect BMI, and have those shoes that so-and-so wore on the red carpet last night, we would finally be "happy."

What can *you* do to stem the tide of "modifiable bodies" and feel better about your own self-image as you face recovery from binge eating disorder? The following tips can help:

- **Focus on health and wellness rather than on achieving a thin ideal.** Know what is good for *your* body (and your body alone), not your beautiful next-door neighbor's body, the instructor at the gym's body, or the body of an actress. Being thin is not entirely a healthy ideal because "thin" is subjective. Do you define it by weight, dress size, waist size? Does it depend on how tall you are? Short you are? You can live on nicotine and caffeine and be "thin," but does that necessarily make you healthy? I believe that if you feel good you will naturally look good. If you consider this chapter as a piece of the bigger whole that is this book, you will realize that moving your body often and feeding your body naturally will help you both feel good *and* look good.

- **Don't buy into arbitrary standards and measurements.** Vanity dress and pants sizing shows that a size is an arbitrary measurement, little more than a marketing ploy. And it makes no sense to try to compete with the bodies of Hollywood actresses and New York models, who have makeup artists and professional photographers to help make them look "perfect." There is no real standard or measurement by which we can measure ourselves because we are all different; be beautiful, proud, and strong in your own unique ways.

- **Focus on health and healthful eating and slow, steady, and sustained change instead of crash cures.** Recovery takes time; health takes time. You can't rush either just because you want to look good right now. Give yourself permission—and time—to recover, eat well, and move more often. Remember that it took years for the disorder to bring you to the point that led to recovery; it is unrealistic, not to mention unwise, to expect overnight results during your recovery.

- **Don't try to fit a square peg into a round hole.** Every day I meet women who have spent their entire adult lives trying to be something—a dress size, a weight, a height—they're not. These are intelligent, strong, successful, independent, beautiful women. And yet Hollywood and the fashion industry have made them feel barely a step above worthless when it comes to their own negative body issues. We have to get to the point where we reject the stick-thin idea of perfection as beauty and celebrate our own unique individual beauty instead. Maybe you are thin by virtue of genes, nature, and good habits; congratulations. But if you're one of the majority of women who aren't naturally thin, don't spend your entire life trying to be; that's a trigger that might have led to your binge eating disorder in the first place. Instead, find things within yourself to be positive about: your laugh, your intelligence, your warmth, your compassion, your sense of humor. Deemphasize the physical and welcome the emotional; be happy for who you are right now and not who you'll be as soon as you look like someone else.

- **Use your voice as an agent of change.** I am consistently encouraged by the way larger-sized women are constantly rewriting the constitution on size issues. For instance, plus-size supermodel and all-around impressive woman Emme is a spokesperson for the Eating Disorders Coalition. Bestselling author and self-esteem expert Jessica Weiner also speaks on behalf of the EDC and National Eating Disorders Association. Tyra Banks and Oprah continue to push the envelope on weight and stereotypes on their respective talk shows, reaching millions of viewers each day with positive, size-conscious messages. So what can you do? Don't think you have to be Miss America, a plus-size supermodel, or talk show host to fight the unrealistic images coming out of Hollywood and the fashion world; speak up about the issue when friends, co-workers, colleagues, or even strangers comment unrealistically about being overweight or overeating. Or, if you're shy, you don't have to say a word; simply be yourself and lead by example.

- **Make your body your affair (ownership and boundaries).** You know how pregnant women always say that people think they have a right to touch their pregnant bellies but that it is really a boundary violation for them? Well, people with anorexia and those individuals who are very overweight also attract comments about their bodies, whereas people in the middle do not attract such commentary. It is as if people think it is okay to discuss the weight and eating of someone at either end of that spectrum. Two former patients come to mind. One, an anorexic woman, while waiting in line at a Burger King had another woman basically start telling her she needed to "eat more." The well-meaning woman came right out and said, "Honey, you need two burgers, not that little salad." The other, an overweight woman, had a person behind her in line remark on the contents of her shopping cart with comments like "Do you really think you need that ice cream?" She felt so bad it triggered a binge. But it wasn't a craving that made her eat; deep down she was angry at the boundary violation.

- **Finally, don't let the bastards get under your skin.** Many of the noxious messages we get from the world come in the form of memes, or little "mind viruses" that bore holes into our brains and get under our skin. They are often "should" statements: You "should" be this way or you "should" be that way. You should be a size 0; you shouldn't have any age spots; you shouldn't have any wrinkles. Well, it's time to eliminate these infectious memes. That's what many outspoken women have done; they have developed Teflon coating that lets the "shoulds" slide right off. Forget about the old Velcro that held fast every meme and set them up as yet another perfectionistic standard you had to live up to. Buy stock in Teflon, not Velcro. *You* set the standards you need to live up to; let other people worry about themselves. Your accountability needs to be to you, not to Hollywood or the beauty industry or even your best friend!

CHAPTER 11

What to Do When
You Hit the Wall

*Having hit a wall, the next logical step is not to bang
our heads against it.*
—STEPHEN HARPER, CANADIAN POLITICIAN

We all encounter barriers every day. The salary cap at work, the
missed promotion last month, the dreaded dieter's plateau,
that second mile we just can't push through every morning, the
courage to ask out that cute guy at work. These barriers can occasionally limit us, but they don't have to define us. And the
best part? Unlike mountains, barriers *can* be removed—you just
have to know how.

You've already come so far; I don't want certain barriers I've
identified over the years to stop you now! Like the rest of life's
greatest accomplishments, sustained recovery requires commitment and vigilance.

Even though we don't look at binge eating disorder in the
same way we look at addictions ("once an alcoholic, always an
alcoholic"), there continue to be a risks of the symptoms

popping up again. If we could live in a vacuum, tightly controlled and not exposed to so many outside forces, perhaps barriers might not be such an issue. Unfortunately, we live in a world chock-full of triggers, and in the case of binge eating disorder, triggers often lead to impediments to recovery. Whether yours is stress or the holidays or seeing a fast-food drive-through window, in our workaday world they are pretty much unavoidable.

Let's look at some effective strategies you can use whenever you feel like giving up on your recovery or feel you are slipping back into bad patterns after a period of doing well.

Identifying the Barriers:
Knowledge Is Key

Rather than having very *non*specific reasons for why certain recovery strategies are no longer working or why you have stopped trying, be *very* specific in identifying what the hurdles are that you have to get over in order to stick with the program and remain well.

Let's review some of the common barriers to recovery to give you a sense of how they can stand in your way. Then you can examine your own situation to see if any of these apply to you and your unique situation.

TIME

For the recovering binge eater, time is the most common barrier—specifically, not having enough of it. "I don't have time to exercise." "I don't have time to self-monitor." "I don't have time to come in for appointments." These are all very common and, I admit, legitimate excuses. But they are still excuses.

In clinical practice, I will ask someone who says he doesn't have enough time for recovery these questions: What are your favorite TV shows? Do you watch your favorite shows in "real time" or TiVo them every week? How many hours per week do you think you spend watching TV?

Let's say he underestimates and says "four hours." Then my comeback is: "Great, we just identified four precious hours that you can devote to your recovery!" My sneaky way of finding time might be a little cheeky, but I can't think of anything better to give up in the name of recovery than TV!

Not only that, but according to *Communications Industry Forecast & Report* by Veronis Suhler Stevenson the average number of hours of TV that adults in the United States watch per year is 1,555 (up from 1,467 in 2000). That translates to almost 65 days—or 2 entire months![1]

Think of how else that time could be put to use—self-monitoring, walking, exercising—doing any number of things to boost your recovery and remove barriers. And if you really *are* glued to the tube, then at least stretch while you are watching or watch one of those exercise shows where you can do aerobics in your living room while the hosts get to do aerobics on some beautiful tropical island!

My point here is that we all have the same number of hours in the day; you can't create more hours but you can *find* time if you only look for it. And excess TV time is a great place to start!

I was doing a guest appearance in one of my junior doctor's weight-loss groups a while back and the topic that night just happened to be "Barriers to Successful Weight Loss." I heard from one of the patients that the junior doctor had warned the group: "Just don't tell Dr. Bulik that you don't have enough time! If Dr. Bulik has enough time, then you have enough time. And believe me, you don't want to hear *that* lecture!"

LACK OF SOCIAL SUPPORT

Are your friends and family supportive of your recovery? Do you have friends and family who are even aware of your recovery?

Do you have a recovery partner, or are you winging this on this on your own?

Another barrier to recovery can be when you feel like you are going it alone. This can be especially tough if the lack of support is coming from someone you love, especially someone you live with. We see this when people are quitting smoking, drinking, or using drugs, and the same holds true for binge eating and weight control. When your spouse or partner becomes a trigger, he or she can be a relapse cue.

How does that work, exactly? Well, let's say that you have successfully managed to break your habit of downing a large bag of chips in front of the TV at night, but your partner, who doesn't admit to his own out-of-control eating (although you still have your sneaking suspicions), insists on engaging in that behavior night after night. You ask him to switch to a healthier food with no success. He sees it as his right to eat whatever he wants in his living room, despite the fact that you're sitting there right next to him and he knows chips are one of your big triggers. Well, this is a tough situation, especially if you want to spend time with him in the evening but just find his eating to be too destabilizing for you.

What are your options?

Of course, the best alternative would be for the two of you to work together toward behavior change. As you can see in the box opposite, couples who live together tend to gain weight together, but couples who try to adopt healthy eating behaviors together are more successful than one partner going it alone.[2] The same holds for binge eating. If you can both tackle your binge eating at the same time, then you can support each other through the difficult times.

If that's not an option, try to convey your concern to your partner and share your thoughts and feelings about the impact that his behavior has on you and your recovery. Depending on the particular dynamics of your relationship, you might be able to work out an alternative that satisfies his need to

THE COUPLE CONNECTION

You know that old saying about how couples tend to start looking more alike the longer they stay together? Well, it turns out that may not be so far off the mark, at least in the weight department. New research has uncovered a connection between how couples who live together tend to gain weight together, and often at the same time.

According to the Weight Watchers Research Institute, which summarized several of the most recently published studies, "in a study that followed newly married spouses for two years, researchers found that the couples had similar BMIs and that marriage was associated with weight gain."[3]

The reasons cohabitating couples gain weight together are many. For one thing, couples who live together often eat at the same times, and the same amounts of food. Married couples often eat more together than they would separately, including at meals out and at home. Finally, singles often want to look as desirable as possible to potential mates; thus they have an added incentive for keeping their weight down. Married or committed couples often have less pressure to "keep up appearances" and thus are more prone to slow and gradual weight gain.

The good news? Researchers also discovered that couples who live and *gain* weight together also have a greater chance of *losing* weight together! An example is cited by the Weight Watchers Research Institute: "A study done in Australia investigated the effects of a sixteen-week lifestyle-modification program for new couples just moving in together. The researchers found that couples who changed their behaviors as a team had better success than those going it alone. The couples lost weight, improved their diet, exercised more and reduced their cholesterol levels."[4]

munch but doesn't send you into a craving tailspin. This could include your buying healthier alternatives like flavored rice cakes or popcorn, for example.

If you offer the alternative snack and he still is not cooperative, then being firm may be your only option. In other words, you matter, too, so you'll just have to make a choice and be clear as you say: "Honey, as much as I would love to spend the evening with you, I just don't feel like I can do it without falling into a binge trap, so I hope you can understand why I can't be with you tonight."

Then you can go into another room and find another source of social support. Go to your favorite chat, blog about your recovery, phone a friend. Any of these healthy options can give you at least some social support (even if it isn't from your partner) and get you away from those high-risk cues. Eventually, either your partner will see your side and reduce his behaviors or you'll just find other times and ways to be together that don't include binge triggers.

Having backup sources of social support for when your primary ones aren't working is critical. They may not be as powerful sources, but in a pinch they can be good stand-ins.

HEALTH

One barrier I often hear about has to do with physical health. Some people find that if something goes wrong with their body they often deprioritize recovery from binge eating disorder to compensate. Recovery from the ailment trumps recovery from binge eating disorder.

Other people will often blame an illness for interfering with their recovery, but from what I have observed it isn't usually the illness per se, but worry about the illness that is to blame. In that case, we're right back to what we have already identified as an emotional cue for binge eating. In reality, there is no better time to get your eating and weight under control than when you are physically ill. That is the time when your body needs you to treat it the best and to eat well to aid in its recovery and not add to the challenges that your body is facing as it is trying to heal.

As an example, one of my patients recently developed a herniated disk in her back. It was around the L4-L5 area and caused radiating pain down her sciatic nerve. Little did she know that this was a syndrome I was very familiar with (having had the same herniation), and one thing I know for sure is that the best way for me to keep the pain away is daily back exercises and walking (not giving up either or both of those activities).

So she had come to me with what she thought was a very well-thought-out plan for how she was going to suspend treatment of her binge eating disorder until her herniated disk got better. Although I could understand her logic, it was completely backward and would have made everything worse, not better. We turned her plan on its head and figured out how we could treat the disk *and* the binge eating disorder with the same interventions.

Luckily, her neurologist had given her an excellent set of exercises and also recommended walking. No coincidence that those two things could be great distractions from her urges to binge, not to mention help her lose weight and maintain that weight loss, which could only be helpful for her disk. When she realized that two battles could be fought with one strategy, she decided that there was no better time to continue with her treatment for binge eating disorder than right now.

MOOD

Back in chapter 4, we talked about the Moody Blues Binger and how mood and appetite are deeply intertwined—even on a chemical level—in our brains. Well, your moods can also play a large role in your motivation to maintain recovery. Recall that depression is often an episodic disorder. You may have periods when your mood is low that last weeks or months, followed by periods of feeling relatively well. Treatment, in the form of psychotherapy or medication, can smooth out those episodes, but if your depression flares up again and remains untreated, those periods of dark moods can rob you of the energy and desire to keep your binge eating under control.

I recall one patient who had had full-blown binge eating disorder since she was a child, but also had battled an episodic mood disorder, as it turned out, also since childhood (although she had never been formerly diagnosed). For years, she noted that dips in that her mood and increases in her binge eating seemed to go hand in hand.

Sometimes it would feel like her mood started slipping first, but other times she would find herself starting to binge again without being aware of any change in mood, and then the dip in mood would follow. The strategy that I took with her was to use each symptom as a warning flag for the other and a loud and clear signal that both needed to be attended to.

Early on, her internal dialogue would be either "I'm just too depressed to care about my binge eating and my weight" or "Binge eating will at least make me feel better for a while." We worked with her to provide new cognitions like "Oh man, I'm binge eating again, I better keep close watch on my mood and see if I need to get back on those meds," and "My mood is slipping, I have to get all of my tools in place now to make sure my binge eating disorder doesn't slip, too." This transformation allowed her to use her symptoms as calls for action rather than signals of impending failure. The more we could help her develop her own personal early warning system, the more in control of her moods and appetite she could feel.

MOTIVATION

What if you just don't feel motivated to continue trying to pursue healthy eating and healthy weight maintenance? Well, the first thing to do is check to make sure all of the other barriers I've mentioned aren't getting in the way and causing that lack of motivation in the first place. But then you have to ask yourself what *is* getting in the way of your taking positive steps toward health. Understanding lack of motivation is all about a careful analysis of what the factors are that motivate you and what the factors are that demotivate you.

I recall another patient who was coming in for weekly therapy for about four weeks. Even though she never missed an appointment, I didn't see any behavior change. She wasn't self-monitoring and wasn't changing her activity patterns, and the binge eating continued. So at first we would spend the beginning of sessions trying to re-create self-monitoring for the week. I would emphasize its importance, but she always seemed to have an excuse for not doing it.

At the fifth session, I realized that this woman was paying for therapy but wasn't really motivated to act on the problem she came to me to address, namely her binge eating disorder. So, we had the conversation about motivation and direction and what we were going to do. What emerged was that she had been highly motivated to change when she found that she could no longer get down on the floor and play with her grandchildren because her weight had gotten so out of control. But soon after she started therapy, her daughter's husband got unexpectedly transferred and they moved three states away. She no longer had the weekly opportunity to see her grandchildren, nor the motivation to get down on the floor to play. She was really coming to therapy just for some weekly company (as she had no other family in the area), and she didn't think it would be likely that she would be seeing the grandchildren any time soon.

She had lost her primary motivation and she was also incredibly (and understandably) sad about losing access to her grandchildren. What we needed to do was begin to structure a new motivation plan that included ways to schedule trips to visit her grandchildren.

Often, we may feel a wave of inspiration come over us, but then it passes, sometimes too quickly for us to act on it. Waiting for inspiration is like waiting for a bus that has stopped running on a particular route; you've got to find the new route if you want to catch the bus and get to where you want to go. Until we truly get a handle on what is slowing us down or how to jump-start the process again, we are faced with the best defense being to examine our thoughts and feelings thoroughly to understand how they influence our behaviors.

Clearing the Hurdles

If you really are struggling, and one or many of the barriers above, or even completely different ones, are operating in your life and you really can't imagine how you are going to be able to keep up with all of the recommendations outlined in this book, here are some ways to get and stay on track during your recovery.

Less Is Sometimes More—Pick One Intervention

Remember what we said about all-or-nothing thinking? People with binge eating disorder tend to think in extremes—either I do everything described in the book or I toss the book and give up trying altogether. When your motivation is lagging, you probably have the energy to do only one thing out of the many I suggest, so pick one that you feel like you can handle and do it consistently.

I remember one patient who had been doing very well, but then his parents got sick, his child started having difficulty in school, and he was in danger of losing his job. He was very clear with me when he warned, "Dr. Bulik, I just can't do it." He explained his situation and I agreed with him. Rather than giving him some meaningless pep talk about being able to be a superpatient and do it all, we tried to find a realistic balance where he could deal with all of the things going on in his life but not completely give up the quest for recovery that he had worked so hard to achieve.

So I asked him of all of the changes he had made, which one did he think he could keep doing consistently until things stabilized. He wisely chose having breakfast every day because he thought he could still keep that structure even if he had to run to the hospital to look after his parents. That one specific intervention became his single therapeutic goal (for the time being).

He put away his all-or-nothing thinking and picked up his all-for-one mentality instead. If he managed to have breakfast every day during this turbulent period, he was still on the path to recovery. The speed of his recovery might be slowed down while he was going through that difficult patch, but the important thing to remember is that he stayed on the recovery path despite the obstacles around him.

This strategy works. You can definitely adjust your pace and adjust your expectations when life gets hairy. Then when things calm down, you can reward yourself by reincorporating other changes and picking up the pace of your recovery.

PRIORITIZE YOU

The Indigo Girls have a great song called "The Girl with the Weight of the World in Her Hands" that perfectly sums up our default setting of having to do everything ourselves if we want it done right. Although this is not entirely a female characteristic, I will say that clinically, although I do see it in men, I see it more often in women. I laughed a few weeks ago when my oldest daughter said to me "Mom, stop it with the self-sacrificing woman routine!" Okay, so even *I* do it sometimes. It is just far too easy to fall into the trap of putting everyone else's needs first, and fearing that everything will fall apart if you don't take the weight of the world on *your* shoulders.

When these perceptions are operating is prime time for some of those damning thoughts like "I *deserve* this ice cream" or "This [the binge] is the only time I have for myself" or "This [binge eating] is the only pleasure I have in life." Well, to be quite frank, if binge eating is the only joy you have in life, then it is time for you to take charge and begin finding some healthier, more worthwhile "you" time so that your life is not so devoid of pleasure and pampering. It may sound like a cliché, but we can do a much better job taking care of others if we take care of ourselves first.

I have an acquaintance who is a master at this technique. I was truly impressed with the manner in which she got her family to rally around her happiness and well-being. She was consistently firm with her children and spouse in asserting that "if Mom's not happy, no one in this family is happy."

The clear implication was that everyone in that family was supposed to work toward keeping Mom happy in order for them all to benefit from her sunny personality and optimisim. Now, this might seem unusually bold and self-serving, but when you think about it, it is a masterful management strategy applied to the entire household: Keep the boss happy and your life will be good! Rather than feeling wrung dry by her kids and husband, she was upbeat and willing to contribute because she was not being taken advantage of. Moms often set the emotional tone for the family. They reap what they sow when they help keep her happy.

There is no honor in being a great multitasker if it drains you of everything you are worth. You were not put on this planet to be a slave. It is okay to deny someone you love something in order to keep yourself whole and sane.

JUST SAY NO

How much of your lack of motivation is due to being completely overwhelmed because of a chronic inability to say no?

Nancy Reagan might have been talking about drugs when she made the phrase "Just say no" famous, but I am talking about your life. I remember when I first tried this out. I was definitely in the "sure, I can do that" category for a long time until my to-do list became so overwhelming that it interfered with my ability to sleep.

In addition to my more than full-time academic job, I was volunteering for all sorts of things, and was always willing to meet with people, talk about their ideas, and help them with whatever came along. Then, after a couple of conversations with my husband that really shook me up, I gradually started to realize that I needed to learn how to say no. I consider this so important that I have started teaching my trainees how to do it.

I think the best example of gracious no-saying that I have ever seen came from a rather high-profile female author who was frequently asked to join nonprofit boards or lend her name to various organizations—and which she invariably had to turn down because of her busy schedule. She had composed a wonderful e-mail that said something along the lines of: "Ms. X truly cares about your organization and its goals, and if she had infinite time and resources would love to support your cause; however, her need to carry on the very important work that she does, which attracted you to her in the first place, is leading her to take some time off from volunteer commitments so that she can pursue her own very important work. Please note that this in no way reflects upon the value of the work *you* are doing, but is about how important it is for her to continue to pursue her own work at this time. She wishes you success in your pursuits."

I just thought that was the kindest and gentlest way to say no. If we transpose what she said into our own lives, it might sound a lot like, "Honey, I know you would like me to drive you to the mall to be with your friends, but it's really important for Mom to get her exercise in today in order for her to stay healthy and happy."

It might feel really hard to do at first—and I'll bet you'll get some twinges of guilt—especially if you get "Susie's mom always drives us places when we ask." In which case your response could be, "Well, maybe Susie's mom can drive you today, too, and then we can work it out in advance so I can drive the next time."

Again, we're not talking about all-or-nothing thinking here. Just permission to say, perhaps for the very first time, "Today I need to come first."

BOOSTER SESSIONS

I just got a tetanus shot. I hate getting tetanus shots because they make my arm hurt for days afterward. But without boosters your immunity from the vaccine wanes, so like many things in life it's just got to be done. The same thing is true with recovering from binge eating disorder. You may have learned all of the skills in this book extremely well the first time through, and you might even be applying them across the board so well that they are improving other aspects of your life. However, a few years from now those memory traces might start to fade, and your excellent recovery skills might start to erode.

Learning these behaviors and techniques is really like learning a foreign language. If you don't speak it for a while, you forget it. But once you pop a language CD on in the car or go to a country where people speak the language, it starts coming back to you. In order to keep your recovery skills sharp, you need to go back to your source materials. Reread chapters, do some self-monitoring, start another recovery blog—in short, be proactive about getting yourself a recovery "booster" shot.

Of course, you should not do this only when you are afraid that you are slipping back into unhealthy behaviors. It is also a great thing to do when you are feeling well! Am I still eating breakfast every day? Keeping up with my exercise? Am I cutting corners? Shaving off time? Your goal is to keep yourself honest and to keep your skills sharp. Those are the keys to maintaining all of the gains that these techniques have the potential to afford you if you stick with them.

Remember, barriers are real; they exist both in our minds and out there in the world. But recovery is vital, so you must be vigilant and persistent in facing these barriers with confidence, knowledge, and skill. Knocking down the obstacles to recovery ensures your reward is not lost. And few things are as rewarding as recovering from binge eating disorder.

Acknowledgments

I would like to thank the following people for their tireless efforts and priceless contributions to the making of this book. First, I offer an apology to my husband for taking on this project without warning him. Second, thanks to Richard Curtis for understanding the importance of the topic and to my editor Jackie Johnson for making it a better piece of work. Finally, I thank all of those who helped me research the background, check the facts, and bring the story of binge eating disorder to life. Among those to whom I am grateful are Tish Rogers Lindberg; Rusty Fischer; Jennifer Shapiro, Ph.D.; Emily Pisetsky; Lauren Reba-Harrelson; Xiaofei Mo, M.D.; the staff of the UNC Eating Disorders Program; and the countless people who have struggled with eating disorders who have shared their stories, challenges, and triumphs.

Notes

Chapter 1   One in Thirty-five: Binge Eating Disorder Is Widespread in America

1. Brody, Jane. "My Binge Year." In *Feed Me!: Writers Dish About Food, Eating, Body Image, and Weight*, ed. Harriet Brown (New York: Ballantine Books, 2009), 175–180.
2. Hudson, J. I., E. Hiripi, H. G. Pope, and R. C. Kessler. "The Prevalence and Correlates of Eating Disorders in the National Comorbidity Survey Replication." *Biological Psychiatry* 2007, 61:348–58.
3. Science Update. "Study Tracks Prevalence of Eating Disorders." National Institute of Mental Health, February 9, 2007. www .nimh.nih.gov/science-news/2007/study-tracks-prevalence-of -eating-disorders.shtml.
4. Berkman, N. D., C. M. Bulik, K. A. Brownley, K. N. Lohr, J. A. Sedway, A. Rooks, and G. Gartlehner. "Management of Eating Disorders." *Evidence Report/Technology Assessment* No. 135 (Prepared by RTI International, University of North Carolina Evidence-based Practice Center under Contract No. 290-02-0016). AHRQ Publication No. 06-E010. Rockville, MD: Agency for Healthcare Research and Quality. April 2006. http://www .ahrq.gov/downloads/pub/evidence/pdf/eatingdisorders/eatdi s.pdf p.9
5. Lerro, Marc, quoted in HealthDay News. "Binge Eating Tops Other Eating Disorders: Survey." *Forbes* magazine, February 1,

2007. http://www.forbes.com/health/feeds/hscout/2007/02/01/ hscout601505.html

6. *Diagnostic and Statistical Manual of Mental Disorders.* 4th ed. Washington, D.C.: American Psychiatric Association, 1994.

7. "Sample USDA Food Guide and the DASH Eating Plan at the 2,000-Calorie Level." *Dietary Guidelines for Americans 2005.* U. S. Department of Health and Human Services. http://www .health.gov/DIETARYGUIDELINES/dga2005/document/html/ chapter2.htm#table1.

8. "Find Specific Information Regarding Eating Disorders in Men and Boys." National Eating Disorders Association, 2008. http://www.nationaleatingdisorders.org/information -resources/men-and-boys.php.

9. "Prescott Tells of Bulimia Battle." http://news.bbc.co.uk/go/ pr/fr/-/2/hi/uk_news/politics/7357008.stm. BBC News, April 4, 2008.

CHAPTER 2   WEIGHT LOSS AND BINGE EATING

1. "Overweight and Obesity: Introduction." Centers for Disease Control and Prevention, March 4, 2008. http://www.cdc.gov/ nccdphp/dnpa/obesity/index.htm.

2. "About BMI for Adults." Department of Health and Human Services. http://www.cdc.gov/nccdphp/dnpa/bmi/adult_BMI/ about_adult_BMI.htm.

3. Karras, Tula. "The Disorder Next Door" *Self* magazine, May 2008, 248–253.

4. Sturm, Roland, and Kenneth Wells. "The Health Risks of Obesity: Worse Than Smoking, Drinking, or Poverty." RAND Corporation, 2005. http://www.rand.org/pubs/research_briefs/ RB4549/index1.html.

5. "Obesity and Overweight: AMH Scientific Position." American Heart Association, 2007. http://www.americanheart.org/ presenter.jhtml?identifier=4639.

6. Simon, G. E., M. Von Korff, K. Saunders, D. L. Miglioretti, P. K. Crane, G. van Belle, and R. C. Kessler. "Association Between Obesity and Psychiatric Disorders in the U.S. Adult Population." *Archives of General Psychiatry*, 2006, 63: 824–30.

7. "Mid-Life Obesity May Raise Dementia Risk: Overweight Women Especially Vulnerable, Researchers Find." Associated Press, 2005. http://www.msnbc.msn.com/id/7667623/.

8. Whitmer, R. A., E. P. Gunderson, E. Barrett-Connor, C. P. Quesenberry, and K. Yaffe. "Obesity in Middle Age and Future Risk of Dementia: A 27 Year Longitudinal Population Based Study." *British Medical Journal*, June 11, 2005, 330: 1360–62.

9. Feigelson, H. S., A. V. Patel, L. R. Teras, T. Gansler, M. J. Thun, and E. E. Calle. "Adult Weight Gain and Histopathologic Characteristics of Breast Cancer Among Postmenopausal women." *Cancer*, July 1, 2006, 107(1):12–21. http://www.cancerproject.org/media/newsletter/octo6/adult_weight.php.

10. "Obesity and Cancer: Questions and Answers." The National Cancer Institute. http://www.cancer.gov/cancertopics/factsheet/Risk/obesity.

11. Olshansky, S. J., D. J. Passaro, R. C. Hershow, J. Layden, B. A. Carnes, J. Brody, L. Hayflick, R. N. Butler, D. B. Allison, and D. S. Ludwig. "A Potential Decline in Life Expectancy in the United States in the 21st Century," *New England Journal of Medicine*, 352(11): 1138–45.

12. "Blood Vessels Show Effect of Fat in Teens." Associated Press, September 21, 2005. http://www.intelihealth.com/IH/ihtIH/EMIHC275/333/20833/432260.html?d=dmtICNNews.

13. "About Eating Disorders." Academy for Eating Disorders. www.aedweb.org/media/Fast_ED_Facts.cfm.

14. Science News: "Binge Eating Disorder." National Institute of Mental Health, June 26, 2008. http://www.nimh.nih.gov/health/publications/eating-disorders/binge-eating-disorder.shtml.

CHAPTER 3   BE COMFORTABLE IN YOUR OWN GENES

1. Hudson, J. I., J. K. Lalonde, J. M. Berry, L. J. Pindyck, C. M. Bulik, S. J. Crow, S. L. McElroy, N. M. Laird, M. T. Tsuang, B. T. Walsh, N. R. Rosenthal, and H. G. Pope Jr. "Binge-eating disorder as a distinct familial phenotype in obese individuals." *Archives of General Psychiatry*, March 2006, 63(3):313–19.

2. Bulik, C. M., P. F. Sullivan, and K. S. Kendler. "Heritability of

Binge-Eating and Broadly Defined Bulimia Nervosa." *Biological Psychiatry*, Dec. 15, 1998, 44(12):1210–18.

3. Reichborn-Kjennerud, T., C. M. Bulik, K. Tambs, and J. R. Harris. "Genetic and Environmental Influences on Binge Eating in the Absence of Compensatory Behaviors: A Population-Based Twin Study." *International Journal of Eating Disorders*, Nov. 2004, 36(3):307 14.

4. Becker, A. E., R. A. Burwell, D. B. Herzog, P. Hamburg, and S. E. Gilman. "Eating Behaviours and Attitudes Following Prolonged Exposure to Television Among Ethnic Fijian Adolescent Girls." *British Journal of Psychiatry* 2002, 180: 509–14.

5. "Study May Lead to New Therapies for Binge Eating Disorder." University of Alabama at Birmingham. *Science Daily*, April 19, 2007; July 8, 2008. http://www.sciencedaily.com /releases/2007/04/070418163657.htm.

6. Boggiano, M. M., A. I. Artiga, C. E. Pritchett, P. C. Chandler-Laney, M. L. Smith, and A. J. Eldridge. "High Intake of Palatable Food Predicts Binge-Eating Independent of Susceptibility to Obesity: An Animal Model of Lean Versus Obese Binge-Eating and Obesity with and Without Binge-Eating." *International Journal of Obesity*, Sept. 2007, 31(9):1357–67.

7. Boggiano, M. M., and P. C. Chandler. "Binge Eating in Rats Produced by Combining Dieting with Stress." *Current Protocols in Neuroscience*. Aug. 2006, ch. 9, unit 9:23A.

8. Treasure, J. L., E. R. Wack, and M. E. Roberts. "Models as a High-Risk Group: The Health Implications of a Size Zero Culture." *British Journal of Psychiatry*, April 2008, 192(4):243–4.

CHAPTER 4   WHAT'S YOUR PROFILE?

1. Grucza, R. A., T. R. Przybeck, and C. R. Cloninger. "Prevalence and Correlates of Binge Eating Disorder in a Community Sample." *Comprehensive Psychiatry*, March–April 2007, 48(2):124–31.

2. Mangweth, B., J. I. Hudson, H. G. Pope Jr., A. Hausmann, C. DeCol, N. M. Laird, W. Beibl, M. T. Tsuang. "Family Study of the Aggregation of Eating Disorders and Mood Disorders." *Psychological Medicine*, October 2003, 33(7):1319–23.

3. Karras, Tula. "The Disorder Next Door" *Self* magazine, May 2008: 248–253. http://www.self.com/health/articles/2008/04/042Idisorder.

4. Keyes, A., J. Brozek, and A. Henschel. *The Biology of Human Starvation.* Minneapolis: University of Minnesota Press, 1959.

5. "144–158: General advice." The Highway Code. http://www.directgov.gov.uk/en/TravelAndTransport/Highwaycode/DG_070309.

6. "Current Distracted Driving Laws." Maryland Department of Transportation, October 2005. http://www.sha.state.md.us/safety/distracted_driving_currentlaws.asp.

7. Stunkard, A., and A. Mazer. "Smorgasbord and Obesity." *Psychosomatic Medicine*, March 1978, 40(2):173–75.

CHAPTER 5   EAT BREAKFAST, HUNGRY OR NOT!

1. Frank, E. *Treating Bipolar Disorder: A Clinician's Guide to Interpersonal and Social Rhythm Therapy.* New York: Guilford Press, 2005.

2. Wyatt, H., G. Grunwald, C. L. Mosca, M. L. Klem, R. R. Wing, and J. O. Hill. "Long-Term Weight Loss and Breakfast in Subjects in the National Weight Control Registry." *Obesity Research*, 2002, 10: 78–82.

3. Purslow, L. R., M. S. Sandhu, N. Forouhi, E. H. Young, R. N. Luben, A. A. Welch, K. T. Khaw, S. A. Bingham, and N. J. Wareham. "Energy Intake at Breakfast and Weight Change: Prospective Study of 6,764 Middle-Aged Men and Women." *American Journal of Epidemiology*, 2008, 167(2):188–92.

4. Croezen, S., T. L. Visscher, N. C. Ter Bogt, M. L. Veling, and A. Haveman-Nies. "Skipping Breakfast, Alcohol Consumption and Physical Inactivity as Risk Factors for Overweight and Obesity in Adolescents." *European Journal of Clinical Nutrition*, November 28, 2007. http://www.nature.com/ejcn/journal/vaop/ncurrent/abs/1602950a.html.

CHAPTER 6   STEALTH SUGARS AND HOW TO RESET YOUR "SWEETSTAT"

1. Goulding, Matt. "The 20 Worst Foods in America." *Men's Health* magazine 2007. http://www.menshealth.com/eatthis/20-worst.foods/10_worst_breakfast.php.
2. Wendys.com.
3. Bk.com.
4. Popkin, Barry M. "The World Is Fat." *Scientific American*, September 2007, 297:88–95.
5. Popkin, Barry M. "The World Is Fat: Obesity Now Outweighs Hunger Worldwide." From a broadcast of *Science Talk*, August 15, 2007.
6. Nielsen, S. J., and B. M. Popkin. "Changes in Beverage Intake Between 1977 and 2001." *American Journal of Preventive Medicine*, Oct. 2004, 27(3):205–10.
7. Popkin, Barry M., et al. University of North Carolina at Chapel Hill. "U.S. Soft Drink Consumption Grew 135% Since 1977, Boosting Obesity." *Science Daily*, September 17, 2004/July 8, 2008. http://www.sciencedaily.com/releases/2004/09/040917091452.htm.
8. Valentine, Judith, Ph.D., CNA, CNC. "Soft Drinks . . . America's Other Drinking Problem." *Wise Traditions in Food, Farming, and the Healing Arts*, Summer 2001, 2(2):12.
9. Bouchez, Colette. "Seven Diet Sins: The Most Common Nutrition Mistakes—and How to Avoid Them." WebMD Weight Loss Clinic—Feature. http://www.medicinenet.com/nutrition/article.htm.
10. "Make Your Calories Count." U. S. Food and Drug Administration. CFSAN/Office of Nutritional Products, Labeling, and Dietary Supplements, November 2006. http://www.cfsan.fda.gov/~ear/hwm/labelman.html.
11. Chan, J., S. F. Knutsen, G. G. Blix, J. W. Lee, and G. E. Fraser "Water, Other Fluids, and Fatal Coronary Heart Disease: The Adventist Health Study." *American Journal of Epidemiology*, May 1, 2002, 155(9):827–33.

CHAPTER 7   OVERCOME YOUR EXERCISE ALLERGY (REVERSE YOUR ACTIVITY AVERSION AND MOVE, MOVE, MOVE)

1. *Health, United States, 2007: With Chartbook on Trends in the Health of Americans.* 567 pp. (PHS) 2007: 10. http://www.cdc .gov/nchs/data/hus/hus07.pdf.

2. "Exercise: 7 benefits of regular physical activity." Mayo Foundation for Medical Education and Research. July 26, 2007. Mayo Clinic.com.

3. Lewine, Edward. "A Film Critic's Windy City Home." *New York Times Magazine*, February 13, 2005. http://www.nytimes.com/ 2005/02/13/magazine/13domains/html.

4. "Dietary Reference Intakes for Energy, Carbohydrates, Fiber, Fat, Fatty Acids, Cholesterol, Protein, and Amino Acids." Food and Nutrition Board. Institute of Medicine National Academies, 2005.

CHAPTER 8   EMBRACE TECHNOLOGY AS THERAPY

1. Tudor-Locke, C. "10,000 Steps a Magic Number?" *Sports Medicine* 2004, 34 (1):1–8.

2. Taylor, C. B., S. Bryson, K. H. Luce, D. Cunning, A. C. Doyle, L. B. Abascal, R. Rockwell, P. Dev, A. J. Winzelberg, and D. E. Wilfley. "Prevention of Eating Disorders in At-Risk College-Age Women." *Archives of General Psychiatry* 2006, 63:881–88.

CHAPTER 9   ONE SIZE DOESN'T FIT ALL OR WHY NOT ALL TREATMENTS ARE EQUAL

1. Insel, Thomas R., M.D. "Fiscal Year 2006 President's Budget Request for NIMH." Appearing before the Senate Subcommittee on Labor-HHS-Education Appropriations, 2006. http://www .nimh.nih.gov/about/budget/fy06_senate_statement.pdf.

2. Berkman, N. D., C. M. Bulik, K. A. Brownley, K. N. Lohr, J. A. Sedway, A. Rooks, and G. Gartlehner. Management of Eating Disorders. Evidence Report/Technology Assessment No. 135 (Prepared by RTI International, University of North Carolina

Evidence-based Practice Center under Contract No. 290-02-
0016). AHRQ Publication No. 06-E010. Rockville, MD: Agency
for Healthcare Research and Quality. April 2006.

3. Brownley, K.A., N. D. Berkman, J. A. Sedway, K. N. Lohr, and
C. M. Bulik "Binge eating disorder treatment: A systematic re-
view of randomized controlled trials." *International Journal of
Eating Disorders* 2007, 40: 337–48.

4. www.oa.org.

5. Adapted from www.nationaleatingdisorders.org.

CHAPTER 10   "YOU CALL *This* FAT?"

1. "Quaid Reveals Eating Disorder." The Daily Dish. *San Francisco
Chronicle.* http://www.sfgate.com/cgi-bin/blogs/sfgate/detail?
blogid=7%3C/cite&entry_id=3482.

2. Engemann, Kristie M., and Michael T. Owyang. "So Much for
That Merit Raise: The Link Between Wages and Appearance."
The Regional Economist (a publication of The Federal Reserve
Bank of St. Louis), April 2005. http://www.stlouisfed.org/
publications/re/2005/b/pages/appearances.html.

3. "Dove® Provides Reality Check on Beauty, Boys and Body Image." Greenwich, CT, Nov. 13, 2007. http://www.rocketxl.com/
dsef/D3.html.

4. Farrell, Timothy M., M.D. Interview by author, April 27, 2008.

5. Boggs, Will, M.D. "Binge eating does not increase bypass surgery risk." Reuters, Jan. 16, 2007. http://www.reuters.com/
article/healthNews/idUSCOL66691120070116.

6. "Safety and health in the horse racing industry." National Institute for Occupational Safety and Health (NIOSH), March 14,
2008. http://www.cdc.gov/niosh/topics/HorseJockey/.

7. Bulik, C. M., A. Von Holle, R. Hamer, C. Knoph Berg, L. Tor-
gersen, P. Magnus, C. Stoltenberg, A. M. Siega-Riz, P. Sullivan,
and T. Reichborn-Kjennerud. "Patterns of remission, continu-
ation and incidence of broadly defined eating disorders during early pregnancy in the Norwegian Mother and Child
Cohort Study (MoBa)." *Psychological Medicine*, Aug. 2007,
37(8):1109–18.

8. Nakashima, Ryan. "New Miss America once battled anorexia." *USA Today*, Jan. 27, 2008. http://www.usatoday.com/news/nation/2008.01-26-2993431164_x.htm.

Chapter 11   What to Do When You Hit the Wall

1. Associated Press, "Study of Americans' Media Use Finds Web Finally Passing Newspapers," Editorandpublisher.com, December 15, 2006. http://www.editorandpublisher.com/eandp/news/article_display.jsp?vnu_content_id=1003522187.
2. Burke, V., T. A. Mori, N. Giangiulio, H. F. Gillam, L. J. Beilin, S. Houghton, H. E. Cutt, J. Mansour, and A. Wilson. "An Innovative Program for Changing Health Behaviours." *Asia Pacific Journal of Clinical Nutrition* 2002, 11 Supplement 3:586–97.
3. "The Link Between Couples and Weight." Weightwatchers.com, May 2007. http://www.weightwatchers.com/util/art/index_art.aspx?tabnum=1&art_id=38871&sc=802.
4. Burke et al., "An Innovative Program."

Index

A Note on the Author

Cynthia M. Bulik, Ph.D., F.A.E.D., is the William R. and Jeanne H. Jordan Distinguished Professor of Eating Disorders at the University of North Carolina at Chapel Hill, where she is also a professor of nutrition in the School of Public Health and the director of the UNC Eating Disorders Program.

A clinical psychologist by training, Dr. Bulik has been conducting research and treating individuals with eating disorders for the past twenty-six years. She received her B.A. from the University of Notre Dame and her M.A. and Ph.D. from the University of California at Berkeley. She completed internships and postdoctoral fellowships at the Western Psychiatric Institute and Clinic in Pittsburgh, Pennsylvania. She developed outpatient, day patient, and inpatient services for eating disorders both in New Zealand and the United States.

Her research has included treatment, laboratory, epidemiological, twin and molecular genetic studies of eating disorders, and body weight regulation. More recently she has begun to explore innovative means of integrating technology into treatment for eating disorders and obesity. She has active research collaborations throughout the United States as well as in Canada, New Zealand, Australia, Norway, Sweden, Finland, Holland, Italy, and Germany.

Dr. Bulik has written over three hundred scientific papers

and chapters on eating disorders and is the author of *Eating Disorders: Detection and Treatment* and *Runaway Eating*.

She is a past president of the Academy for Eating Disorders, past vice president of the Eating Disorders Coalition, and associate editor of the *International Journal of Eating Disorders*. Her academic life is balanced by being a happily married mother of three and an ice dancer.